DATE DUE			

DAYS OF
JUDGMENT

Days of Judgment

THE WORLD WAR II WAR CRIMES TRIALS

Isobel V. Morin

THE MILLBROOK PRESS
BROOKFIELD, CONNECTICUT

Photographs courtesy of U.S. Army (courtesy Harry S. Truman
Library): pp. 8, 42; Harry S. Truman Library: pp. 17, 30, 37
(all photos by Charles Alexander); Bettmann Archive: pp. 12,
19, 24, 27, 33, 40; UPI/Bettmann: pp. 28, 47, 51, 53, 57, 69,
80, 83, 85, 99, 112; National Archives: pp. 62, 65; Douglas
MacArthur Memorial Library: pp. 74, 77, 90

Library of Congress Cataloging-in-Publication Data
Morin, Isobel V., 1928–
Days of judgment : the World War II war crimes trials
by Isobel V. Morin.
p.   cm.
Includes bibliographical references and index.
Summary: A history of the international war crimes trials
that followed World War II, examining the reasoning that
led to the charges, the conduct of the trials, and their out-
comes, with biographical information on the defendants.
ISBN 1-56294-442-8 (lib. bdg.)
1. War crimes trials.   2. World War, 1939–1945—Atrocities.
I. Title.
D803.M67   1995   940.54′05—dc20   94-11295   CIP   AC

Published by The Millbrook Press, Inc.
2 Old New Milford Road, Brookfield, Connecticut 06804

Contents

DAYS OF
JUDGMENT

Former prisoners of a Nazi concentration camp wait to be taken to a hospital in April 1945, after their camp was liberated by the Allies.

Chapter One

GERMANY
—
SPRING 1945

The young American G.I. shook his head as he looked at the piles of rotting corpses. "These guys just starved to death," he said. He repeated the words over and over. "They just starved."

It was April 1945. The place was Buchenwald, one of the infamous concentration camps that Nazi Germany had set up to house political prisoners. The American troops who entered Buchenwald found a grisly scene. The horror of the masses of unburied bodies was matched by the sight of the living prisoners—the ragged, filthy, vermin-infested human skeletons whose stench rivaled the stomach-turning odor of rotting flesh that hung over everything. One veteran war correspondent, sickened by the discovery, wrote that Buchenwald would stink through the years of history.[1]

The scene at Buchenwald, near the town of Weimar (the site of Germany's ill-fated experiment in democracy during the 1920s and early 1930s), marked the climax of a tragedy that had been unfolding for more than thirty years in Europe. The tragedy began on June 28, 1914, in the city of Sarajevo, in the Balkan Peninsula, with the assassination of Archduke Francis Ferdinand, the heir to the Austro-Hungarian empire. The assassination stemmed from the desire of militant Serbian nationalists to unite the Balkan region under Serbian control. The conflict that followed the assassination resulted in a bloodbath of unprecedented scope: about 8.5 million deaths among military personnel, and another 13 million civilian deaths.[2]

After World War I, the victorious Allies, angered by Germany's attack on Belgium (a neutral country) and by reports of German atrocities against civilians, wanted to punish Kaiser Wilhelm II as a war criminal. (Before that, war itself, however dreadful its consequences, had been regarded as a legitimate enterprise.) The Kaiser, who fled to Holland in 1918, was never put on trial, however. A few Germans were tried in German courts for war crimes, but most were found innocent, and those who were convicted received light sentences.

The aftermath of World War I also brought a wave of antiwar sentiment as people realized the enormity of the catastrophe. A League of Nations was formed to guarantee future peace. There were attempts to limit armaments and to outlaw weapons such as poison gases. In 1928, representatives of fifteen nations, including the United States, France, Great Britain, Germany, and Japan, signed the Kellogg-Briand Pact (sometimes called the Treaty of Paris). The pact, or treaty, condemned war as a way of settling international disputes, but it provided no penalties for starting a war. Eventually many other nations signed the treaty.

The national leaders who condemned war in 1928 didn't know that the period of peace they enjoyed was only an intermission after the first act in the twentieth-century tragedy of world wars. A new and deadlier second act was to begin shortly, one that would engulf both Europe and Asia in an even greater bloodbath.

Europe's march toward war began in 1933, when Adolf Hitler and his National Socialist German Workers' party (called the Nazi party) gained control of the German government and Hitler became a dictator. Soon afterward, the Nazis opened the first concentration camps to confine Gypsies and other "undesirables" who didn't satisfy the Nazi idea of racial purity, as well as communists, socialists, and other political enemies of the Nazi regime.

The Jews were the prime target in the Nazi drive to preserve the purity of the German "master race." Hitler and his fellow Nazis blamed the Jews for Germany's problems after its defeat in World War I. The Nazi government passed laws barring Jews from holding public office or working as civil servants, teachers, journalists, doctors, or lawyers. The Nazis took away the Jews' German citizenship and prohibited them from marrying German citizens. They seized Jewish property, burned Jewish synagogues, and brutally attacked many Jews. Some Jews managed to escape to other countries, where they told their grim stories to the outside world, which was often reluctant to listen, much less to believe. Others, who were not so lucky, were rounded up and put into concentration camps.

Not satisfied with controlling Germany, the Nazis soon set their sights on neighboring countries. Early in 1938, Germany annexed Austria, and it took over parts of Czechoslovakia a short time later. Although these acts were widely condemned, the memory of the recent world war was so fresh that few wanted to risk military action against the culprit. Germany's invasion of Poland, on September 1, 1939, was the last straw, how-

Nazi troopers arrest a group of Jewish men.

ever. Great Britain and France declared war on Germany, marking the official opening of World War II.

As Germany overran much of Europe in the late 1930s and early 1940s, the Nazis viciously attacked those who dared to resist German rule, sometimes carrying out reprisals against entire towns for the acts of a few members of resistance groups. They mistreated or murdered prisoners of war, and sent both civilians and war prisoners to work as slave laborers in German war industries. As the war widened in scope and ferocity, the Nazis tried to exterminate the entire Jewish population of the conquered territories and to kill or enslave the Slavs (Poles, Russians, Czechs, and other eastern Europeans).

From time to time the Allied leaders issued stern warnings that those who committed such crimes would be punished severely. In 1943 a United Nations War Crimes Commission was set up to gather evidence against war criminals. No firm plans for punishing them were made, however. The war was far from over, and the immediate goal was victory.

In the spring of 1945 the scene at Buchenwald was repeated in other concentration camps as the British, Americans, and other Allies swept across Nazi-occupied territory in western Europe and into Germany itself. Bergen-Belsen. Dachau. Erla. Nordhausen. Mauthausen. The eyewitness stories of the horrors of these camps, accompanied by graphic photographs, shocked the civilian population of the United States, which had not experienced the Nazi brutalities firsthand. A tidal wave of outrage swept over the country: Those who committed these evil deeds must be brought to justice!

Chapter
Two

THE ROAD TO
NUREMBERG

By the spring of 1945, Germany was on the brink of total collapse. The Allies now had to make final plans for the postwar period. The United States, Great Britain, and the Soviet Union had already agreed to divide Germany into three zones, each of which would be occupied by one of these countries. They later invited France to occupy a fourth zone.

Germany's surrender in May 1945 required a number of other decisions regarding the defeated enemy. One of the most important questions was what to do with the leading Nazis. Thinking that the top Nazis might use a trial to defend their vicious doctrines, some Allied leaders wanted to execute them on the spot. This idea was quickly abandoned, however. The Allies decided that in a civilized society there should be no executions without a trial.

The decision to put the top Nazis on trial raised other questions. One was what kind of trial should be held. Trials of the Nazi leaders in the existing civil courts didn't seem practical. Many of their crimes extended beyond any single country's jurisdiction. Also, the civil courts in many areas were so thoroughly contaminated by Nazism that they seemed incapable of making just decisions. The Allies therefore decided to establish an International Military Tribunal (IMT) to try the Nazi leaders. The IMT would consist of four judges and four alternates representing the United States, Great Britain, the Soviet Union, and France.

Warring nations often use military tribunals to deal with acts such as spying and sabotage. These tribunals can usually provide swift justice, since their rules are more flexible than those that civil courts must follow. The idea of an Allied tribunal was controversial, however. Many thought that a trial in which both the prosecutors and the judges belonged to the winning side was inherently unfair, but there seemed to be no alternative. There was no existing international court to try people for war crimes. Moreover, it might be hard to persuade neutral countries to provide judges for an international trial. Regardless of any shortcomings of an Allied tribunal, the major criminals must be brought to justice. Their crimes were so heinous that it was unthinkable to allow them to go unpunished.

The Allies also had to decide what acts should be considered war crimes for which the Nazi leaders could be tried. Military personnel who were guilty of plunder, rape, or murder were clearly subject to criminal charges under the existing international agreements. However, the traditional concepts of war crimes didn't include the actions of the officials who ordered such atrocities or the industrial and financial leaders who created and bankrolled the war machinery. Moreover, the existing international agreements didn't apply to crimes committed against one's own people.

[15]

Faced with the possibility that the worst criminals might escape punishment, the Allies decided to charge the top Nazis with two new categories of war crimes. One category was crimes against peace, which involved starting or waging aggressive wars or taking part in a conspiracy to commit these acts. The other category was crimes against humanity, which included such acts as the enslavement or murder of civilians both before and during the war, and the persecution of groups of people on political, racial, or religious grounds. (The deliberate attempt to exterminate entire groups is called genocide.)

There were problems with this approach. One was that in the past, war had not generally been considered a crime punishable under international law. Even the terms of the 1928 Kellogg-Briand agreement didn't specifically make aggressive war a crime. Some objected to the idea of punishing people for acts that were not considered crimes when they were committed. Another problem was that, given the shifts in national boundaries as a result of previous wars, it could be difficult to determine whether a military action was a war of aggression or simply an attempt to win back one's own lost territory. The Allies believed, however, that the Nazi invasions of other countries were clearly wars of aggression, and that aggressive warfare and other atrocities were crimes, whether or not international law labeled them as such.

The Allies also decided that a position as a government official shouldn't free a person from individual responsibility for war crimes. The fact that someone committed crimes under orders from superiors could be considered in determining the punishment, however. The Allied agreement regarding the trial of major German war criminals was set forth in a document called the London Charter, issued in London on August 8, 1945.

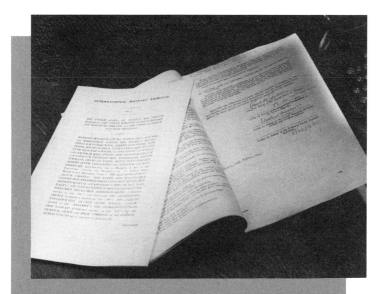

The indictment, or formal charges, brought against Nazi leaders at the International Military Tribunal at Nuremberg. It was signed by representatives of the United States, France, Great Britain, and the Soviet Union.

Next came the question of which Nazis should be tried before the IMT. Opinions varied both within one country's leadership and among the Allies. However, some viewpoints predominated. The British generally wanted to try only a small group of the most notorious criminals. The French and Russians wanted a series of trials that would include Germany's financial and industrial leaders as well as high-ranking military and civilian officials. The Americans, in a display of crusading zeal, wanted to put the entire Nazi regime on trial. It was clearly impossible to put every Nazi on trial, however, even if the proceedings were spread out among a number of separate trials. Some weeding out was necessary.

A few obvious names had to be omitted. As far as anyone could tell, Hitler had killed himself in his underground bunker in Berlin shortly before that city fell to the Russians. Hitler's propaganda minister, Joseph Goebbels, also killed himself in Berlin. Another top Nazi official, Heinrich Himmler, who was responsible for the operation of the concentration camps, killed himself after the British captured him.

Many leading Nazis were in custody, however. Most of them were in American or British hands. Rudolf Hess, one of Hitler's earliest supporters, had been held in Great Britain since May 1941, when he flew to Scotland in an attempt to negotiate peace with the British. Toward the end of the war, many Nazi officials fled to the south and west, preferring to take their chances with the British or Americans rather than risk being captured by the advancing Soviet armies. For example, Hermann Goering, the fat, jovial head of the German Air Force, surrendered to the Americans in Austria.

By the end of August 1945, Allied prosecutors had picked twenty-four persons to stand trial before the IMT. The defendants represented a cross section of the military, political, and economic leadership of Nazi Germany. As expected, both Goering and Hess were on the list. Both had been second in command to Hitler at different times. There was some question regarding Hess's sanity, but the Russians, convinced that Hess had tried to make peace with Great Britain to clear the way for Germany's invasion of Russia in June 1941, wanted him tried anyway.

The list included four members of the German High Command in addition to Goering. They were Admiral Karl Doenitz, who headed the remnants of the German government after Hitler's death; Admiral Erich Raeder, a former head of the German Navy; Field Marshal Wil-

Adolf Hitler strolls with Air Force chief Hermann Goering in 1934, before the outbreak of the war.

helm Keitel, chief of staff of the German Army; and Colonel-General Alfred Jodl, one of the signers of the surrender papers.

Eleven defendants were former high-ranking officials in the Nazi government. Three of these were diplomats: Joachim von Ribbentrop, Germany's wartime foreign minister; Constantin von Neurath, who was foreign minister from 1932 to 1938 and "Protector" of Bohemia and Moravia after Germany took over these Czech provinces; and Franz von Papen, Germany's wartime ambassador to Turkey, who had helped Hitler to gain power in 1933. Two, Hjalmar Schacht and Walther Funk, were former ministers of economics. The remaining six were Martin Bormann, a member of the Council of Ministers for the Defense of the Reich, who was also Hitler's personal secretary; Ernst Kaltenbrunner, a top official of the German security police; Robert Ley, head of the German Labor Front (the Nazi version of a labor union); Wilhelm Frick, a former minister of the interior, who also governed parts of occupied Europe; Albert Speer, minister of armament and munitions; and Fritz Sauckel, plenipotentiary general for the utilization of labor (a high-sounding title that meant Sauckel directed the Nazi forced-labor program).

Four defendants in addition to Neurath and Frick had governed portions of Nazi-occupied territory. They were Hans Frank, governor of occupied Poland; Alfred Rosenberg, governor of the other occupied territories in eastern Europe; Arthur Seyss-Inquart, governor of the Netherlands; and Baldur von Schirach, the wartime governor of Vienna and former head of the Hitler Youth, an organization that trained German boys to be loyal Nazis.

The remaining defendants were Julius Streicher, a former Nazi party leader and newspaper publisher; Gustav Krupp, the former head of an armaments firm; and

Hans Fritzsche, an official in the Nazi propaganda ministry.

Some of these choices seemed questionable. Martin Bormann, a leading Nazi party official, had been one of Hitler's most notorious associates. However, Bormann had been missing since the final days of the battle for Berlin. There had been reports that he was killed while trying to escape from the Russians. He would be tried anyway.

Gustav Krupp may have been named by mistake. The Krupp firm had been heavily involved in supplying arms to the Nazi war machine, but when the elderly Gustav Krupp had a stroke in the early 1940s, his son Alfried took over the running of the business. After the prosecutors found out that Gustav Krupp was bedridden and senile, they tried to substitute Alfried as a defendant. The judges refused to allow this, but agreed to postpone action against Gustav Krupp. The elder Krupp, who never recovered enough to stand trial, died in Austria in 1950.

Hans Fritzsche seemed too unimportant to be tried as a major war criminal. His main contribution to the German war effort was a series of radio propaganda broadcasts called "Hans Fritzsche Speaks." German listeners often sarcastically referred to the program as "His Master's Voice." Many suspected that this relatively minor official was either a stand-in for his dead superior, Joseph Goebbels, or that the Russians wanted him listed because he was their prisoner. The only other Russian prisoner on the list of defendants was Admiral Raeder, also included as a defendant at the Russians' request.

The prosecutors also included seven German organizations as defendants. They were the Armed Forces General Staff and High Command, the Reich Cabinet, the Nazi Party Leadership Corps, the Gestapo, the SA, the SD, and the SS. The Gestapo got its name from a contraction of the German words for "secret state police." The letters SA stood for German words meaning "storm troopers," SD for "security service," and SS for "protection squad." These last four groups were responsible for most of the prewar and wartime atrocities under the Nazi regime. Under the London Charter, if any organizations were found to be criminal in nature, their members could be judged guilty of war crimes based on their membership. This provision was added to speed and simplify future war crimes trials. It was controversial, however. Many thought it was unfair to charge people with crimes simply because they belonged to an organization.

The charges against the defendants were written down in a formal document called an indictment. The charges were divided into four main counts. Count One was called "The Common Plan or Conspiracy," Count Two was "Crimes Against Peace," Count Three was "War Crimes" (acts such as plunder, rape, and murder), and Count Four was "Crimes Against Humanity." All twenty-four defendants were charged with criminal conspiracy. Thirteen were charged under all four counts. They were Goering, Ribbentrop, Hess, Rosenberg, Frick, Sauckel, Speer, Funk, Krupp, Neurath, Seyss-Inquart, Keitel, and Jodl. The remaining eleven were charged under one or two counts in addition to the conspiracy charge.

The last question was where to hold the trial. The Soviets wanted it held in Berlin. However, Berlin had been so heavily damaged in the final days of the war that no suitable building was available. Also, Berlin (although governed jointly by the United States, Great Britain, France, and the Soviet Union) was in the Soviet occupation zone, making it an undesirable site from the viewpoint of the other Allies. (There were already visible cracks in the Allies' solidarity.)

The German city of Nuremberg had also been heavily damaged, but its Palace of Justice was still standing. So was the adjoining prison, which had ample room to house the defendants. Besides, a covered walkway connected it to the Palace of Justice, making it easier to guard the prisoners during the trial. There was an appealing symbolism in holding the trial at Nuremberg, where the annual Nazi party rallies had been held and the laws that stripped Jews of their German citizenship had been issued. It had another advantage from the viewpoint of the Americans. Nuremberg was in the American occupation zone.

In October 1945 the defendants (except for the missing Bormann) were given copies of the charges against them and offered help in getting lawyers to defend them. There was a mad scramble for suitable housing as the four judges and their four alternates, along with an army of lawyers, translators, and other military and civilian personnel, descended on the devastated city of Nuremberg. The stage was set for what promised to be one of the most important trials of the twentieth century.

The Palace of Justice in Nuremberg was closely guarded during the trials.

Chapter Three

NUREMBERG

THE INTERNATIONAL MILITARY TRIBUNAL

Nuremberg's Palace of Justice was crowded on November 20, 1945, as white-helmeted American military police led twenty sallow and somewhat seedy prisoners into the courtroom to face trial for war crimes.

Four of the original twenty-four defendants were missing. Bormann still hadn't been found. (He was never found. Although he was presumed to have died in Berlin, this was never established.) Krupp was still confined to bed in his Austrian home. Ley had killed himself in his cell shortly after receiving his copy of the charges against him. Kaltenbrunner was in a nearby American army hospital with suspected meningitis. He later recovered enough to join his fellow defendants in court.

There was one other missing defendant. He was neither named in the indictment nor present in court, yet in a real sense Germany's late *Fuehrer,* Adolf Hitler, was on trial for all the crimes committed in pursuit of his goals of racial purity and world dominance. Although the defendants generally avoided blaming him for the Nazis' crimes, every aspect of the trial pointed to Hitler as the master criminal behind the Nazi conspiracy.

Most people expected the trial to be brief. After all, most of the defendants had played prominent roles in the Nazi regime. It should be fairly easy to convict them of war crimes. Moreover, the London Charter expressly stated that the tribunal was not to be bound by technical rules of evidence, but was to apply an "expeditious and nontechnical procedure." Those who expected a brief trial were wrong, however. The trial lasted a little over nine months. Almost a hundred witnesses testified, and thousands of official documents, affidavits, motion pictures, and still photographs were presented as evidence. The trial transcript covered almost seventeen thousand pages. After the trial ended, the judges took a month to reach their verdicts and another day and a half to announce them. It wasn't until October 1, 1946, that the defendants learned their fate.

When the trial opened, nothing in the defendants' appearance suggested that these men had once ruled much of Europe. Most of them showed the effect of several months' confinement in prisons or internment camps. One journalist described them as "a drab assortment of mediocrities."

The defendants ranged in age from thirty-nine to seventy-three. Most were in their fifties or sixties. The oldest, Neurath, was an old-school diplomat whom Goebbels once described as "a weak sneak." The youngest, Schirach, alternated during the trial between remorse and defiance. At one point an exasperated Goering, who had tried to bolster up Schirach's courage, called him a young weakling.

The Nuremberg courtroom: Judges, seated at right, face the defendants, who are guarded by white-helmeted military police. Teams of lawyers sit at the tables in the foreground; the witness stand is on the far side of the room.

The IMT defendants. Front row, left to right: Goering, Hess, Ribbentrop, Keitel, Rosenberg, Frank, Frick, Streicher, Funk, Schacht. Second row: Doenitz (partly visible on the left), Raeder, Schirach, Sauckel, Jodl, Papen, Seyss-Inquart, Speer, Neurath, Fritzsche. Kaltenbrunner was not in the dock when this picture was taken.

As the trial progressed, observers noticed differences among the defendants, many of whom had seemed completely nondescript at its opening. There was the white-haired aristocrat, Papen, whom people at Nuremberg called the Silver Fox; the former diplomat, Ribbentrop, who often sat with his head held back and his eyes closed; the mousy little peasant, Sauckel; and the stiff, close-mouthed bureaucrat, Frick, incongruously dressed in a checked sport jacket. There were the military defendants, struggling to maintain their rigidly erect posture. There was the financier, Schacht (whose unlikely middle name of Horace Greeley was a product of his father's stay in the United States before his birth), sitting with his back to his fellow defendants, and the tearful, pasty-faced Funk, who had once edited a business journal.

Many observers found some of the accused men particularly unlikable. Streicher, the editor of a viciously anti-Semitic newspaper, had a history of sex offenses and a habit of leering at the women in the courtroom. One journalist contemptuously summed him up as "a dirty old man." His lawyers questioned Streicher's mental condition, but the doctors who examined the editor found him fit to stand trial. Frank, the so-called Butcher of Poland, had tried to kill himself after his capture but succeeded only in partially paralyzing one hand. Most observers doubted the sincerity of Frank's abject expressions of remorse. Rosenberg, the author of dense, unreadable Nazi propaganda that even Hitler called "illogical rubbish," struck one British diplomat as "a ponderous lightweight." Kaltenbrunner, a tall man with a scarred, pockmarked face, seemed to one journalist to resemble a vicious horse.

Other defendants were viewed more favorably by observers. The architect, Speer, a handsome, cultured man in his early forties, impressed both the prosecutors and judges. Seyss-Inquart, an Austrian who walked with a slight limp, was cheerful and congenial in his dealings with the other defendants. Fritzsche, whose slight build gave him a youthful appearance, was especially popular with his fellow defendants, who were convinced that he was on trial only to satisfy his Russian captors, who had squeezed a confession out of him during a period of solitary confinement in a Moscow prison.

Above: Keitel (left), Kaltenbrunner (center), and Rosenberg confer during the trial. Below: Some of the defendants at lunch during the trial. Goering (left foreground) chats with Doenitz; to Doenitz's right are Funk and Schirach. The man to Goering's left is not identified.

Goering and Hess stood out from the others almost immediately. From the outset, Goering tried to capture center stage. He continually postured in the courtroom, laughing, gesturing, and making audible comments about the testimony. Hess, on the other hand, spent much of the trial staring vacantly into space. His only signs of life were his frequent complaints of stomach cramps and occasional outbursts that seemed unrelated to what was going on in the courtroom. Before the trial, Hess claimed to have lost his memory. However, shortly after the trial opened, during a court session on his competence to stand trial, Hess surprised everyone by announcing that he had faked a loss of memory for tactical reasons, which he did not describe. Many observers thought that Hess belonged in a mental hospital, but the judges decided to allow him to stand trial.

Although the court was a military tribunal, most of the judges and alternates were civilians with experience as judges in their own countries. Both the American judge, former U.S. Attorney General Francis Biddle, and his alternate, John J. Parker, had served as federal appeals court judges. The chief prosecutors were also prominent lawyers with experience in criminal trials. The American chief prosecutor, U.S. Supreme Court Justice Robert Jackson, had also been a U.S. solicitor general and attorney general.

Each of the Allied prosecution staffs was responsible for presenting the evidence on one of the four main charges. The Americans took the job of proving the conspiracy charge. The British handled the charge of crimes against peace. The French and Russians divided the charges of conventional war crimes and crimes against humanity, with the French handling those committed in western Europe and the Russians handling those committed in eastern Europe.

The Americans led off with their presentation of evidence on the existence of a criminal conspiracy, which Justice Jackson saw as the heart of the case against the defendants. It was the common thread that tied together the members of this diverse group. Jackson hoped to use the conspiracy charge to convict the defendants of crimes that had been committed both in Germany and other countries throughout the twelve years of Nazi rule.

The notion of a criminal conspiracy, which is generally found only in the British and American criminal justice systems, is a useful means of convicting both those who actually commit criminal acts and the ringleaders who order the crimes. Where a criminal conspiracy exists, all persons who knowingly take part in it are guilty of all its crimes, even though they didn't personally commit them and may not even have known about them. However, the prosecutors must establish an individual's criminal intent, which is not always easy.

Justice Jackson's opening statement was one of the high points of the trial. In a voice that sometimes broke with emotion, the American jurist summarized the case against the defendants. He began by saying:

> The privilege of opening the first trial in history for crimes against the peace of the world imposes a grave responsibility. The wrongs which we seek to condemn and punish have been so calculated, so malignant, and so devastating, that civilization cannot tolerate their being ignored, because it cannot survive their being repeated.

He then traced the Nazis' rise to power, their oppression of the German people, their aggression against Germany's neighbors, and their wartime atrocities. He con-

Chief U.S. prosecutor Robert Jackson opens
the case against the defendants.

cluded with a plea to the judges on behalf of civilization, the real complaining party before them. He said:

> Civilization asks whether law is so laggard as to be utterly helpless to deal with crimes of this magnitude by criminals of this order of importance. It does not expect that you [the tribunal] can make war impossible. It does expect that your juridical actions will put the forms of international law, its precepts, its prohibitions and, most of all, its sanctions, on the side of peace, so that men and women of good will, in all countries, may have "leave to live by no man's leave, underneath the law."

The prosecutors built their case largely on the Nazis' own records. They read excerpts from these records in a seemingly endless recital of incredible brutalities. Chilling though the readings were, those who heard them became bored by the repetition. Every so often, however, the evidence was shocking enough to catch the audience's attention.

Early in the trial the Americans showed a film of the concentration camps at Dachau, Buchenwald, and Bergen-Belsen. Allied military photographers had taken the motion pictures when British and American troops entered these camps. Few of those who watched the film remained unmoved at the grisly sight of the masses of unburied bodies and the starving, filthy survivors. During its showing, Schacht (who had been imprisoned in German concentration camps for several months after he turned against the Nazis) sat with his back to the screen.

The French and Russian evidence seemed unnecessary after the Americans and British had finished. Hadn't the Nazi leaders' guilt already been established?

However, both France and the Soviet Union wanted to add their scenes to the grim morality play unfolding before a worldwide audience.

The French gave evidence of the forced labor of more than three million Belgians, Dutch, and French in support of the German war effort. They also described the wholesale seizure of machinery, fuel, and food without regard to the needs of the civilian populations, the killing of more than thirty thousand hostages, and the torture and murder of thousands of concentration camp inmates.

The Soviet story was, if anything, more shocking than the French presentation. The Russians described how millions of Soviet prisoners of war, herded together in open enclosures without food or shelter during the harsh Russian winter, froze or starved to death, while special groups of SS men who followed the German troops into the battle areas murdered suspected Communist party officials on the spot. The Soviets also produced evidence dealing with the infamous death camps in eastern Europe: Auschwitz, Maidenek, Chelmno, Sobibor, and Belsec. These were the places to which millions of Jews, Gypsies, and other "undesirables" were sent to be exterminated. The Soviets showed captured German photographs of these camps and a film illustrating what the camps looked like when Soviet troops entered them. There were no ragged, starving survivors. The Germans had moved the inmates to other locations before the Soviet armies arrived. There were other horrors, however. The sight of the mutilated bodies, the instruments of torture, the gas chambers, the ovens for burning the bodies, and the piles of clothing and human hair (which had been saved for future Nazi use) was too much for most of the defendants, who hid their eyes to avoid looking at the hideous spectacle.

Goering alone pretended indifference, yawning and glancing at a book while the film was being shown.

After the film, four survivors of the death camps testified. One woman told of the murder of newborn infants, who were often thrown alive into the ovens along with the corpses from the gas chambers. At the end of this testimony Doenitz's lawyer asked, "Didn't anybody know anything about any of these things?" Doenitz shook his head and shrugged, while Goering answered with a cynical "of course not." But Jodl snapped, "Of course somebody knew about it!"

This conversation touched on the unspoken question that hung over the trial. How could atrocities on such a colossal scale have taken place without the help, or at least the knowledge, of large numbers of Germans? Justice Jackson took pains in his opening statement to point out that the German people weren't on trial, but they were believed by many to share in their leaders' guilt. This question still troubles Germany half a century later.

In fact, no one's hands were entirely clean. The Russians brazenly insisted on charging the Germans with the murder of thousands of Polish officers in Poland's Katyn Forest in 1941, even though it was later shown that they themselves committed this crime in 1940. (At that time the Russians occupied part of Poland under a secret agreement with Nazi Germany for Poland's dismemberment.) Also, in an attempt to destroy Germany's ability to fight, the British and Americans repeatedly bombed German cities, killing large numbers of civilians. The Allies justified these raids as retaliation for German air bombardment of cities and said that, while they didn't intend to kill innocent persons, in a modern total war civilian deaths are inevitable. At the time, moreover, the Allies were more interested in punishing Nazi war criminals than in examining their own consciences.

Guarded by two MP's, Schirach confers with his lawyer.

The defense attorneys were German lawyers of varying ability. Eight of them were former members of the Nazi party. Although some defendants chose their own lawyers, the court staff had to assign German lawyers to defend others. Many German lawyers were understandably reluctant to defend notorious Nazis before their conquerors. There was one big advantage in accepting the role of defense attorney, however. The defendants' lawyers got lunch every day, and weekly rations of goods such as soap and cigarettes from the American military post exchanges. These items were enormously valuable at a time when most consumer goods, including food, were hard to get in Germany.

Shortly before the trial opened, the defense lawyers joined in questioning its legality. They argued that international law didn't recognize war as a crime and that a tribunal consisting only of representatives of the winning side couldn't be fair. The judges promptly rejected these arguments because the London Charter forbade any challenges to the tribunal's existence or membership.

In many cases the evidence of a defendant's guilt was overwhelming. The defense attorneys did the best they could for their clients, however. Most of the defendants either denied knowledge of criminal acts or claimed to be obeying orders. (Under the terms of the London Charter, this latter defense couldn't be used to establish innocence, although it could be a mitigating factor in imposing punishment.) Some defendants made half-hearted apologies, while others blamed one another or the dead Himmler for the atrocities.

Goering stubbornly tried to justify all of Nazi Germany's actions. For two and a half days Goering, prompted by his lawyer's questions, described the Nazis' rise to power and Germany's preparations for war. His poise and seeming openness while offering evidence of his own part in the Nazi drive toward world power made a favorable impression on those who heard his testimony. Justice Jackson, who had held the audience spellbound during his opening statement, proved surprisingly clumsy in his cross-examination of the glib Goering, who soon had the American prosecutor tied in knots. One of the British prosecutors had to come to Jackson's rescue.

Speer also gave a candid recital of his own part in the Nazi war effort. He admitted his share of responsibility for the "inconceivable catastrophe" that had befallen Germany and the rest of the world. He also described his growing awareness that Germany was losing the war, his loss of faith in the *Fuehrer* he had once revered, and his attempts to counteract Hitler's orders for the destruction of Germany's means of survival in the final days of the war.

On August 31, 1946, the trial ended and the judges began to discuss their verdicts. The tribunal's rules required three votes to convict a defendant and impose a sentence. Thus a tie vote would result in an acquittal. Some cases gave the judges little trouble, while others were decided only after extended debate. Often the Russian judge cast the lone dissenting vote.

The courtroom was crowded again on September 30, 1946, as the tribunal assembled to announce its judgment. The judges made it plain that they considered aggressive war a crime. It was, moreover, "the supreme international crime." The judgment also declared that Germany's attacks on European countries beginning with the invasion of Poland were aggressive wars. The conspiracy charge had given the judges considerable trouble, but eventually they decided that although more than one criminal plot had existed, under the terms of the London Charter the conspiracy charge applied only to crimes against peace. The judges decided further that their jurisdiction over crimes against humanity was limited to acts committed on and after September 1, 1939, the day Germany invaded Poland. (War crimes, needless to say, could be committed only during a war.) This meant that the Nazis' prewar atrocities were outside the tribunal's authority.

The court acquitted three organizations: the Reich Cabinet, the Armed Forces General Staff and High

Judge Francis Biddle of the United States
confers with Lord Justice Lawrence of Great
Britain (in glasses). Biddle's alternate,
Judge John J. Parker, is on his left.

Command, and the SA. The first two groups were not really "organizations" in the general sense of the word. Moreover, they were so small that their members could more easily be tried as individuals. In fact, seventeen members of the Reich Cabinet and five members of the High Command were among the defendants at Nuremberg. (A few defendants belonged to both groups.) The SA, a notorious gang of thugs who "protected" the Nazis during their push for political power, was virtually eliminated by a 1934 purge of the Nazi party. Thus the SA itself was not involved in crimes that fell under the tribunal's jurisdiction.

The judges found that the SS, SD, Gestapo, and the Nazi Party Leadership Corps were criminal organizations. There was ample evidence of the criminal nature of these groups, whose members committed most of the Nazi atrocities. However, the judges decided that a conviction based on membership in a criminal organization would require proof that the member knew about the organization's criminal nature and voluntarily took part in its criminal activities. They also decided that honorary, clerical, and similar members who didn't engage in criminal conduct couldn't be charged with a crime based on their membership.

Once it was decided that the conspiracy charge applied only to crimes against peace, the judges acquitted fourteen defendants of conspiracy because the evidence wasn't sufficient to prove that they were involved in Germany's war plans. Eleven of the fourteen were convicted of other crimes. The remaining three (Schacht, Papen, and Fritzsche) were completely acquitted. Many of the prosecutors had thought all along that the cases against these three men were weak.

Six defendants (Goering, Ribbentrop, Frick, Neurath, Keitel, and Jodl) were found guilty of all four

Papen (left), Schacht (center), and Fritzsche were acquitted.

counts. The aged Neurath was sentenced to fifteen years in prison. The others received death sentences. Neurath's attempts to minimize the Nazi brutalities in Bohemia and Moravia while he governed these Czech provinces (and possibly his advanced age) were mitigating circumstances that resulted in his comparatively light sentence. The judges found no mitigating circumstances regarding the other five, however.

Goering had been one of the most powerful men in Germany during the Third Reich. As Jackson put it during his closing argument, Goering "stuck his pudgy thumb in every pie." Ribbentrop, as Germany's foreign minister, was involved in every important move toward war. Moreover, during the war he ordered German diplomats to push for the deportation of Jews to the extermination camps. As Armed Forces Chief of Staff, Keitel not only figured prominently in German war plans but also ordered such atrocities as the execution of hostages, the murder of Soviet prisoners of war, and the punishment without trial of suspected resistance fighters. Rosenberg, one of the earliest members of the Nazi party, was heavily involved in the Nazi atrocities in eastern Europe while he was Reich Minister for the Occupied Eastern Territories. As Chief of the Operations Staff of the High Command, Jodl reported directly to Hitler on operational matters and thus knew about most if not all the atrocities committed by the German armed forces. He also personally ordered some atrocities and passed along his superiors' orders for others.

Seven defendants who were acquitted of conspiracy were convicted of other charges and sentenced to death. They were Kaltenbrunner, Frank, Bormann, Frick, Sauckel, Seyss-Inquart, and Streicher. All were convicted of crimes against humanity. All except Streicher were also convicted of conventional war crimes.

Kaltenbrunner's position as head of the Reich Main Security Office virtually guaranteed a death sentence. That office was responsible for the activities of the Gestapo, SD, and SS. As governors of occupied territories, Frank, Frick, and Seyss-Inquart were heavily involved in the Nazi crimes in these areas. Sauckel's part in the forced-labor program, which resulted in many deaths from starvation and overwork, was enough to condemn him to death. Bormann had been heavily involved in the Nazi persecution of Jews, the use of slave labor, and the mistreatment of war prisoners. Streicher's anti-Semitic rantings were considered crimes against humanity even though they weren't directly tied to any actual violence against Jews.

In addition to Neurath, three others (Funk, Schirach, and Speer) escaped the death penalty despite their conviction of crimes against humanity. All three were acquitted of the conspiracy charge. Funk, who was convicted of crimes against peace, war crimes, and crimes against humanity, was sentenced to life imprisonment. The judges held that in spite of his high-level positions, Funk was never a dominant figure in the Nazi leadership. They regarded this as a mitigating factor in determining his sentence. Schirach was convicted of crimes against humanity because while he was governor of Vienna, he agreed to the deportation of Viennese Jews to eastern Europe, where many of them ended in the Nazi death camps. He received a twenty-year sentence. His comparative youth and impressionable nature may have contributed to this relatively light sentence. Speer was convicted of war crimes and crimes against humanity because of his involvement in the forced-labor program. However, his attempt to block Hitler's "scorched earth" order at the end of the war was a mitigating circumstance that resulted in a twenty-year sentence.

Admiral Raeder, who took part in the German war plans until his retirement in 1943, was convicted of conspiracy as well as crimes against peace and war crimes. He received a life sentence. Admiral Doenitz, acquitted of conspiracy but convicted of crimes against peace and war crimes, received a ten-year sentence, the most lenient prison term given to any of the Nuremberg defendants. The judges regarded evidence that Doenitz followed the international rules in his treatment of British war prisoners as a mitigating circumstance that lessened his punishment.

Hess was found guilty of both conspiracy and crimes against peace, but acquitted of war crimes and crimes against humanity. He received a life sentence. The sentence was a compromise. Initially the Russian judge wanted him hanged, the British and Americans wanted life imprisonment, and the French judge thought twenty years was a sufficient punishment. Eventually the Russian judge went along with the British and Americans to impose a life sentence on Hitler's former deputy.

On the afternoon of October 1, 1946, the day of judgment for the individual defendants, the eighteen convicted men were brought into the courtroom one at a time to hear their sentences. Then they were taken back to the prison, where those who received death sentences were separated from the others. The entire sentencing took only forty-five minutes.

Although the tribunal's judgments were not subject to review, the Allied Control Council (a four-member body with representatives from the United States, Great Britain, France, and the Soviet Union), which had overall responsibility for governing occupied Germany, could reduce the sentences. The lawyers for all the convicted men except Kaltenbrunner filed such appeals, but the members of the Council, after reviewing the evidence, refused to change the sentences.

Early in the morning of October 16, 1946, ten of the condemned men were hanged in the prison gymnasium. The eleventh man managed to cheat the hangman. Shortly before midnight on October 15, 1946, Hermann Goering killed himself by cyanide poisoning. Although some suspect that a sympathetic guard may have smuggled the poison into Goering's cell, this has never been established.

The seven men sentenced to prison terms remained at Nuremberg until July 1947, when they were taken to Spandau Prison, in the British sector of Berlin, to serve the balance of their sentences. Any reduction in those sentences required the agreement of all four members of the Allied Control Council. In 1954 the members of the Council agreed to release the feeble Neurath, who had a heart attack two years earlier. Neurath died in 1956. In 1955, Raeder, who was also in poor health, was released. Raeder died in 1960. Funk, who was confined to bed during much of his last three years in prison, was released in 1957. He, too, died in 1960. The others served their full sentences. Doenitz was freed in 1956, and Speer and Schirach were released in 1966. After that, only Hess remained in Spandau. Despite many appeals for clemency, the Soviet representatives on the Allied Control Council never agreed to his release. He committed suicide in Spandau in 1987 at the age of ninety-three.

In his final report to President Harry Truman in October 1946, Justice Jackson wrote:

> Of course, it would be extravagant to claim that agreements or trials of this character can make aggressive war or persecution of minorities impossible, just as it would be extravagant to claim that our federal laws make federal crime impossible. But we cannot doubt that they strengthen the bulwarks of peace and tolerance. . . . By the Agreement and this trial we have put International Law squarely on the side of peace as against aggressive warfare, and on the side of humanity as against persecution. In the present

An official U.S. Army hangman readies
a noose for a war-crimes execution.

depressing world outlook it is possible that the Nürnberg trial may constitute the most important moral advance to grow out of this war.[3]

Future events would show whether Jackson gave an accurate summary of the trial's results.

The Nuremberg trial wasn't perfect. No human undertaking is. Despite the strenuous efforts of the judges to be fair to the defendants, some of the sentences may have been overly harsh, at least in comparison with the lesser punishments that others who seemed equally guilty received. Why, for example, was Sauckel sentenced to hang, while Speer, who gave Sauckel his orders, was sentenced to only twenty years in prison? Perhaps a few defendants were convicted unfairly. Was Hess insane? Did Streicher's anti-Jewish ravings cause anyone to mistreat or murder Jews? Many have wondered about these and other questions. Still, the written record of the International Military Tribunal at Nuremberg remains as a permanent reminder of the crimes that shocked the world during World War II.

Chapter Four

OTHER WAR CRIMES TRIALS IN GERMANY

Even before the war ended, it was clear that if the Allies hoped to bring the bulk of the Nazi war criminals to justice, more than one trial would be necessary. In fact, there were many such trials. Each member of the occupying powers held war crimes trials in its own German occupation zone. Also, many European countries tried both their own people and captured Germans for crimes committed during the Nazi occupation.

The Allies originally considered holding several international trials of major German war criminals. However, the international trial at Nuremberg was the only such trial that took place in Germany. This was mainly due to the breakdown of the wartime alliance between the Soviet Union and the Western democracies. The alliance had never been firm. The conflicting political philosophies of democracy and communism almost guaranteed mutual distrust and hostility. Held together by military necessity while the fighting continued, the alliance began to crumble as soon as the war was over.

As the international trial at Nuremberg progressed, the Americans in particular turned against the idea of further international trials. Justice Jackson was especially opposed to the idea. Jackson, who never fully trusted the Russians, had always been lukewarm toward a tribunal that included a Russian judge. Eventually Jackson's opinion prevailed.

While no subsequent international trials were held in Germany, the Americans held two different types of trials in the U.S. occupation zone. After the International Military Tribunal at Nuremberg finished its work, American judges in that city presided over twelve trials involving 177 high-level German officials who were accused of the broad categories of war crimes defined in the London Charter, such as crimes against peace and crimes against humanity. In addition, U.S. military commissions held a number of trials of persons accused only of conventional war crimes.

Most of the members of the twelve Nuremberg tribunals were state court judges brought from the United States for these trials. Some of them served on more than one tribunal. Brigadier General Telford Taylor, who had been one of the American prosecutors during the international tribunal, was in charge of the prosecution during the twelve trials of the so-called second tier officials. A few other prosecution officials from the international tribunal stayed on in Nuremberg for the later trials, but most of the prosecutors were new. In contrast, most of the defense attorneys during the later trials had represented defendants before the international tribunal and were thus experienced in this type of defense.

Eleven of the twelve later Nuremberg trials involved multiple defendants, who were grouped into categories to speed and simplify the proceedings by reducing the need to repeat the same evidence over and over. (Some

Brigadier General Telford Taylor (in uniform) led the prosecution at the later Nuremberg trials.

individuals fit into more than one category. They were tried with the group that seemed to best fit their case.) Three trials dealt with SS officials, three with industrial leaders, three with doctors, lawyers, and other high-ranking government officials, and two with military leaders. The remaining trial involved only one defendant. He was Erhard Milch, a former field marshal in the German Air Force and an official of Albert Speer's Central Planning Board. In April 1947, Milch was convicted of exploiting slave labor and sentenced to life imprisonment. His sentence was later reduced to fifteen years.

The first trial, in the so-called Medical Case, began in December 1946. The twenty-three defendants were doctors and other medical personnel. The charges included responsibility for cruel and often deadly experiments on concentration camp inmates, prisoners of war, and others. In August 1947, the judges acquitted seven defendants and convicted the remaining sixteen. Five of those convicted were sentenced to life in prison, and four were sentenced to lesser prison terms. The remaining seven received death sentences. They were hanged after the U.S. military government upheld the sentences and the U.S. Supreme Court refused to review the case.

In the so-called Justice Case, fourteen judges, prosecutors, and officials of the German Ministry of Justice were accused of using the German justice system to persecute, enslave, or murder large numbers of Jews and others. In December 1947, the judges acquitted four defendants and convicted the other ten, who received prison sentences ranging from life to five years.

The trial in the Pohl Case involved eighteen SS officials, including Oswald Pohl, who headed the SS unit that ran the concentration camps. The charges included responsibility for the mistreatment of concentration

Karl Brandt, Hitler's personal physician, was sentenced to death for ordering cruel and deadly experiments on prisoners.

camp inmates, many of whom were forced to work in SS-operated businesses in or near the camps. In November 1947, the judges acquitted three defendants and convicted the other fifteen. Four of those convicted, including Pohl, were sentenced to death, and the other eleven received prison sentences ranging from life to ten years. In August 1948, after hearing additional arguments, the judges reduced three prison sentences and commuted one death sentence to life imprisonment.

The RuSHA Case was so named because some of the defendants were officials of the SS Main Race and Resettlement Office (or RuSHA, from its German name), one of the agencies that tried to preserve Germany's racial purity. The charges against the fourteen defendants included the persecution and murder of Jews throughout Europe. In March 1948, the judges acquitted one defendant and convicted five of membership in the SS with knowledge of its criminal activities. The five were immediately freed because their time in prison while awaiting trial was held to be enough punishment. The remaining eight, who were convicted of all charges, received prison sentences ranging from life to ten years.

The Einsatzgruppen Case dealt with one of the Nazis' most heinous crimes—the massacre of between one and two million Jews, Communist officials, and others in the Soviet Union. The twenty-two defendants were either commanders or other officers of the extermination squads *(Einsatzgruppen)* that carried out the slaughter. The principal defendant, Otto Ohlendorf, who commanded one of these units, had testified about the activities of the extermination squads in January 1946 before the international tribunal at Nuremberg. During his own trial, Ohlendorf admitted that his unit had killed about ninety thousand Jews, including children. In April 1948, the judges convicted all of the defendants. They sentenced Ohlendorf and thirteen others to death. Two defendants received life sentences, and five received lesser prison terms. One defendant, who was convicted only of membership in the SS, was sentenced to the time already spent in confinement.

Three of the Nuremberg trials involved executives of huge German industrial combines that had helped Germany to rearm and wage war against its neighbors. The charges included plunder and the use of slave labor in the firms' business operations. Both the percentage of convictions and the length of the sentences in these cases were lower than those resulting from the other trials.

In the Flick Case, involving six officials of the Flick coal and steel combine, three defendants were acquitted and the others received sentences ranging from seven to two and a half years. The seven-year sentence was imposed on Friedrich Flick, the head of the combine, who was convicted of economic plunder, knowingly using slave labor, and knowingly aiding the SS in its criminal activities. The I. G. Farben Case involved twenty-three officials of the giant Farben combine, a prominent supplier of chemicals used in the German armaments industry. The judges acquitted ten defendants. The remaining thirteen received sentences ranging from eight years to one and a half years. The judges imposed the longest prison terms (two eight-year terms and one seven-year term) on three defendants who were directly responsible for the operation of a synthetic-rubber factory that the firm built next to the Auschwitz death camp so it could conveniently use the inmates as slave workers.

The principal defendant in the Krupp Case was Alfried Krupp, who ran the family-owned armaments firm after his father suffered a stroke in the early 1940s. (The Allies had attempted without success to try him before the International Military Tribunal at Nuremberg after they realized that his father, who was listed on the indictment, wasn't able to stand trial.) In July 1948, the judges acquitted one of the twelve defendants and convicted the others of using slave labor. Six of these, including Krupp, were also convicted of plunder. The sentences were relatively mild, however, ranging from the time already spent in prison to twelve years. Alfried Krupp was one of those receiving a twelve-year sentence. In addition, the judges ordered the confiscation of all his property.

The trial in the Hostage Case involved one field marshal and nine generals who commanded troops in southeastern Europe. They were charged with responsibility for the killing of thousands of civilians, many of whom were hostages who were executed in reprisal for the acts of irregular troops (called partisans) who fought against the Nazi rulers. In February 1948, the judges acquitted two defendants, imposed life sentences on two others, and sentenced the rest to lesser prison terms.

The trial in the High Command Case involved thirteen field commanders and staff officers who were charged with planning and waging aggressive wars, ordering the killing and mistreatment of prisoners of war, and participating in the deportation and other abuses of enemy civilians. In October 1948, the judges acquitted two defendants. The other eleven received prison sentences ranging from three years to life.

The Ministries Case involved twenty-one leading officials of various government agencies who were accused of a variety of crimes, including planning and waging aggressive war, murdering and mistreating prisoners of war, and committing atrocities against civilians both in Germany and elsewhere. The trial itself lasted about ten months, and the judges took another five months to reach their judgments, which they announced in April 1949. There were two acquittals and nineteen convictions on various charges. The sentences, which were the last imposed by the Nuremberg tribunals, ranged from less than four years to twenty-five years in prison. These sentences contrasted sharply with the far harsher sentences imposed in the Medical Case almost three years earlier.

Late in 1945, the U.S. Army began holding trials at the former concentration camp at Dachau for persons accused of conventional war crimes. There were almost five hundred such trials involving about seventeen hun-

A concentration camp victim lays her hand
on the shoulder of one of the defendants at
the Dachau trial, identifying him as one who
committed atrocities at the camp.

dred defendants. More than half of the trials, involving over a thousand defendants, were for atrocities committed at concentration camps in the American occupation zone. About two hundred trials, involving about six hundred defendants, dealt with the killing of Americans, mainly fliers whose planes were shot down over Germany. The remaining trials dealt with a variety of other conventional war crimes.[4]

The earliest of the trials for atrocities at concentration camps involved forty guards and other officials of the Dachau camp who were accused of crimes committed there. The judges convicted all of them. They sentenced thirty-six to death and the remaining four to prison terms ranging from ten years to life. In late 1947, in one of the last U.S. Army trials, twenty defendants were tried for atrocities committed at Nordhausen. Four were acquitted, and only one of those convicted received a death sentence. The contrast in the sentences imposed as a result of the Dachau and Nordhausen cases reflected a common pattern in all the American trials: In general, the earliest trials resulted in the harshest sentences.

One of the most controversial of the trials held at Dachau involved seventy-three members of an SS tank regiment who were accused of the murder of more than seventy American soldiers near the town of Malmédy, Belgium, in December 1944. The Americans had surrendered, but the SS troops, who had orders to take no prisoners, killed all of them. The trial in the Malmédy Case, which took place from May to July of 1946, was far from a model of criminal justice. The seventy-three men, who were tried as a group, wore numbered tags around their necks for identification. Although the group as a whole had clearly committed a war crime, the evidence against individual defendants wasn't always convincing. Nevertheless, the judges found all of the defendants guilty after less than two and a half hours of discussion, an average of less than two minutes per defendant. They sentenced forty-three men to death, twenty-two to life imprisonment, and the rest to prison terms ranging from ten to twenty years.

The verdicts and sentences in the Malmédy Case (as in all the American trials) were reviewed by others before being carried out. The Army's review of the verdicts in the Malmédy Case, which took more than a year to complete, resulted in a recommendation in October 1947 that only twenty-five of the death sentences be upheld. Later reviews of the Malmédy Case by other army personnel and outside groups resulted in recommendations for further sentence reductions. Some of the reviews focused on the methods used to obtain evidence rather than the evidence itself. (There had been unsubstantiated claims that the suspects in the Malmédy Case were tortured to get their confessions.) In the end, none of the Malmédy defendants was hanged. By the late 1950s, all of them had been freed.

The outcome of the Malmédy Case was typical of what happened in the aftermath of the American trials. Most of the sentences were eventually reduced, sometimes substantially. The reductions were at least partly due to a vigorous campaign by American and German groups against both the sentences and the trials.

The Americans who objected to the trials had a variety of reasons for their opposition. Americans of German ancestry worried about relatives and friends being tried as war criminals. American business executives objected to the notion that running a business could be considered a crime. Others believed that the Soviet Union, not Germany, had been the real enemy all along.

The Germans had never completely agreed with the Allies' decision to hold war crimes trials. Many Germans, including some who detested Nazism, viewed the trials as an unfair form of "victor's justice." Opponents of capital punishment called for the commutation of the death sentences. Former Nazis and Nazi sympathizers, who had reason to fear the trials, joined in the clamor against them. The German opposition to the sentences intensified during the negotiations that led to the formation in 1949 of the Federal Republic of Germany, a combination of the American, British, and French occupation zones. The Russian zone became the Communist-dominated German Democratic Republic that same year.

In January 1951, the Americans, who still retained authority over those convicted in the American war crimes trials, granted clemency to many of the convicted men. Most of them (including ten who had been sentenced to death) were either paroled immediately or had their sentences reduced. Alfried Krupp was among those who were released from prison. Krupp was also given back his confiscated property. Others who received clemency included all of the surviving defendants in the Medical Case, almost half of those convicted of other atrocities in concentration camps, four of those convicted in the Justice Case, and almost all of the SS men convicted in the Einsatzgruppen Case.

The 1951 clemency decisions did not extend to seven men condemned to death for their participation in mass killings. The seven included Oswald Pohl, Otto Ohlendorf, and three other commanders of the Einsatz-gruppen, and two officials of the Buchenwald concentration camp. Despite strenuous efforts by large numbers of Germans to save their lives, the seven were hanged in June 1951.

During the 1950s, the Americans reduced the sentences of additional war criminals and released others on parole. In May 1958, the last of the men convicted in the American war crimes trials were freed from-prison. One had been convicted of atrocities at Nord-hausen. The other three had originally been sentenced to death in the Einsatzgruppen trial.

The American effort to punish German war criminals, which began as a sweeping crusade, ended in what many regarded as a dismal failure. Only a few of those suspected of war crimes were severely punished, and many of the worst criminals escaped punishment completely.

There were several reasons for what happened. To begin with, the Americans may have taken on too big a job. The trial of large numbers of suspected war criminals was a lengthy process. As the wartime hatreds subsided, Americans who had initially demanded retribution against those who committed atrocities began to seek reconciliation with their former enemy. The advent of the Cold War also influenced American attitudes toward Germany. (The term "Cold War" refers to the period of hostility between the Communist countries and the Western democracies that resulted in an arms race but not another actual war.) Instead of an enemy to be defeated, Germany became a friend and ally in the struggle against the new enemy. If a few criminals went unpunished, it seemed a small price to pay for peace and security.

Perhaps what happened was inevitable, even without the Cold War. Blanket amnesties are often given in the aftermath of wars as former enemies try to achieve reconciliation. Still, the millions who had suffered under Nazi rule must have wondered why the Americans, who had done so much to crush the oppressors, allowed so many of them to get away with murder.

A U.S. ship explodes during the Japanese raid on
Pearl Harbor, December 7, 1941. The surprise attack,
which drew the United States into World War II,
became a symbol of treachery to many Americans.

Chapter Five

PEARL HARBOR, HAWAII
——
DECEMBER 7, 1941

Most Americans were enjoying a leisurely Sunday when the news broke. Japanese warplanes had bombed the U.S. naval base at Pearl Harbor, Hawaii, destroying several ships that lay at anchor. Other reports of Japanese bombings of American-held islands in the Pacific Ocean soon followed. Guam. Midway. Wake. The Philippines. A shocked country reacted angrily to the news of Japan's "sneak attack," which took place without a declaration of war. In fact, the attack occurred while Japanese diplomats were in Washington on what was supposed to be a peace mission. The next day, when President Franklin D. Roosevelt announced to a joint session of Congress that December 7, 1941, was "a date which will live in infamy," few Americans disagreed.

Reports of Japanese aggression had been coming out of Asia for ten years, beginning in 1931, when a group of Japanese army officers arranged for the bombing of railroad tracks in Mukden, in the Chinese province of Manchuria. Japan then used the bombing as an excuse for a Japanese takeover of the province. After the League of Nations condemned the takeover, Japan withdrew from that organization.

The war ministers had always held great power in the Japanese government, as did the army high command, which chose the war ministers from the ranks of the army officers. Several times during the 1930s, war-minded army officials forced the resignation of prime ministers who opposed their policies. When this tactic failed to work, they resorted to violence. Two Japanese prime ministers who opposed the militarists were assassinated during this period, and a third survived an attempted assassination.

Once the militarists gained the upper hand in the Japanese government, they consolidated their power by propaganda and intimidation. They included military training and official government propaganda in the Japanese public school programs. They also imposed tight censorship on the press and radio, while the Kempeitai, an organization of military police often called Thought Police, arrested and imprisoned those who opposed the war ministry's policies.

In 1937, Japan's conflict with China widened into full-scale war. Americans, many of whom sympathized with China, reacted with dismay to Japanese conquests of more and more Chinese territory. In December 1937, American anger erupted when Japanese planes bombed and sank the American river gunboat *Panay* in China's Yangtze River. The *Panay* was anchored near the Chinese city of Nanking to remove Americans who wanted to get away from the Japanese troops who were closing in on the city. The Japanese government apologized for the sinking and paid for the loss of the *Panay,* but by that time Americans were further enraged by reports that the Japanese troops who conquered Nanking had gone

A terrified baby cries in the ruins of a Shanghai
train station after a Japanese air attack in 1937.

on a six-week rampage of rape, plunder, and murder—an atrocity that became known as the Rape of Nanking.

As the 1930s ended, relations between the United States and Japan steadily worsened. In 1940, concerned about Japan's military buildup, the United States stopped the shipment of gasoline, iron, steel, and rubber to Japan. The United States hoped to convince Japan to end its war against China, but the action hardened Japanese resistance to American demands. In the fall of 1941 the Japanese prime minister, Prince Fumimaro Konoye, who favored reaching some sort of agreement with the United States, resigned. A new Japanese government was formed, with Lieutenant General Hideki Tojo (a career army officer who became minister of war in 1940) as prime minister. Tojo instructed Japanese diplomats to continue their negotiations with American officials. However, the new Japanese prime minister, convinced that American actions threatened Japan's economic survival, immediately began making plans for war against Great Britain, the Netherlands, and the United States.

After attacking Pearl Harbor and other Pacific military bases, the Japanese quickly overran the Philippines and most of Southeast Asia, including the British stronghold of Singapore, on the Malay Peninsula. The war in the Pacific was savage and brutal. After American and Filipino troops surrendered to the Japanese invaders in the Philippines, Americans were shocked and outraged by reports of Japanese mistreatment of American prisoners of war during the so-called Death March on Bataan Peninsula. The forced march to Japanese prison camps resulted in the death of about ten thousand American prisoners from lack of food and medical care. Toward the end of the war, while American troops were closing in on Manila in their campaign to free the Philippines from Japanese control, large numbers of Japanese sailors in Manila went on a rampage, raping, torturing, and killing thousands of Filipino civilians before the advancing Americans cornered and killed them. This rampage was called the Rape of Manila.

People in many areas of the Pacific suffered at the hands of the Japanese during the war. But for most Americans, Pearl Harbor remained the central symbol of Japanese treachery. They believed that those responsible for it must be made to pay.

Chapter
Six

THE ROAD TO
TOKYO

In August 1945, while Americans rejoiced over Japan's surrender, officials in Washington were busy making decisions regarding the defeated enemy. One was what to do about Japanese war criminals.

Although the Allies had been gathering evidence of Japanese war crimes for some time, there were no firm plans for the punishment of Japanese war criminals at the time of Japan's surrender. The London Charter, signed a few days earlier, applied only to the treatment of major German war criminals. It seemed likely, however, that something along the lines of the London Charter would govern the treatment of those suspected of major war crimes in the Far East.

Shortly after Japan's surrender, the Allies named General Douglas MacArthur, the wartime commander of the Allied forces in the southwest Pacific, to head the Allied occupation of Japan. MacArthur's title as occupation leader was Supreme Commander for the Allied

Foreign minister Mamoru Shigemitsu (with cane) and General Yoshijiro Umezu led the Japanese delegation to the official surrender ceremony aboard the U.S.S. *Missouri* on September 2, 1945. Both were later charged with war crimes.

Powers, commonly referred to as SCAP (an acronym that stood for both MacArthur and his occupation staff). During his stay in Japan, MacArthur represented both the United States and its Pacific war Allies (Great Britain, China, the Soviet Union, France, the Netherlands, Australia, New Zealand, Canada, India, and the Philippines). As an American general he was under the authority of the Joint Chiefs of Staff, who supervised the entire American military forces. As SCAP he was under the authority of the Far Eastern Commission, an Allied group that had overall responsibility for the Japanese occupation.

When MacArthur arrived in Japan at the end of August 1945, he had orders to arrest and detain suspected war criminals. SCAP ordered the first arrests on September 11, 1945. About forty suspects were on the list, including former prime minister Tojo and several members of Tojo's wartime cabinet. Subsequent arrests included many other high-ranking Japanese officials, including a few with close ties to Emperor Hirohito. In early December 1945, SCAP ordered the arrest of two men who were among Hirohito's closest advisers: Marquis Koichi Kido, Keeper of the Privy Seal (a member of the Emperor's personal staff); and Prince Konoye, who had served three terms as prime minister. By the end of 1945, there were scores of suspected war criminals in Tokyo's Sugamo Prison.

Arresting the suspects was fairly easy. Few Japanese officials had fled or gone into hiding to avoid arrest. A number of officials committed suicide, however. (Many of them killed themselves in fulfillment of the Japanese military code of honor, which required a person who had disgraced himself by a significant failure to atone for the offense by suicide.) Tojo and Konoye both tried to kill themselves. Konoye succeeded, but American doctors saved Tojo's life by an emergency blood transfusion.

The Allies divided Japanese war criminals into three classes: Class A—those who committed crimes against peace; Class B—those who ordered or permitted conventional war crimes; and Class C—those who actually committed conventional war crimes. Class A suspects would be tried before an international military tribunal, while Class B and C suspects could be tried in other courts.

In December 1945, SCAP established an International Prosecution Section (IPS) to deal with the Class A suspects. Joseph B. Keenan, a former U.S. Justice Department official, headed the new section. At first, most of Keenan's staff were Americans. Other Allied prosecutors joined the group later. However, the Americans took pains to make sure that the Tokyo trial remained largely an American show.

One of IPS's first jobs was the drafting of a charter for the International Military Tribunal for the Far East (IMTFE). Although the IMTFE's charter generally followed the London Charter, there were a few differences based on the initial experience in setting up the Nuremberg tribunal and the differing circumstances in Japan. Instead of four judges and four alternates, the IMTFE's charter provided for between six and eleven judges, with no alternates. MacArthur was to appoint the judges from names submitted by each of the Pacific war Allies. The proceedings of the Tokyo trial were conducted only in Japanese and English, instead of the four languages used in the Nuremberg trial. (English was the usual language for seven of the eleven Allies in the Pacific war, and SCAP strongly urged the other four to name prosecutors and judges who spoke English.) Because a preliminary investigation failed to show the existence of any Japanese organizations comparable to the Nazi SS and Gestapo, the Tokyo tribunal's charter contained no provision for the trial of organizations.

Another important difference from the London Charter dealt with jurisdiction. Whereas the Nuremberg tribunal could try persons accused of any of the three major categories of crimes (crimes against peace, crimes against humanity, and conventional war crimes), the Tokyo tribunal could try only those charged with crimes against peace. (The IMTFE could also try such persons for conventional war crimes and crimes against humanity, as long as they were accused of at least one count of crimes against peace.)

The prosecution staff also had to gather evidence against the major war crimes suspects. This proved to be an extremely difficult job. The staff was hampered by their lack of knowledge of the Japanese language, culture, and history, and by the destruction of large amounts of documentary evidence. Some documents had been destroyed by the American bombings, while the Japanese deliberately destroyed others during the two-week period between Japan's surrender and the arrival of the occupation forces.

Once the evidence had been gathered, the prosecutors had to choose the persons who would be tried before the Tokyo tribunal. As at Nuremberg, this required some weeding out. There were hundreds of major war crimes suspects, and IPS wanted to pick a representative group of military and civilian leaders from those who were involved in each of Japan's acts of aggression between 1931 and 1945. Some former officials were eliminated from consideration because of their advanced age or poor health. Others, especially business and financial leaders who didn't hold high government office, were eliminated because of a lack of evidence tying them to crimes against peace. Eventually the prosecutors chose twenty-eight defendants, representing a cross-section of Japan's military and governmental leaders during the 1930s and 1940s.

As expected, Tojo headed the list, along with eleven men who had held prominent offices in the Japanese government at the time of the Pearl Harbor attack. Four were members of Tojo's cabinet: the finance minister, Okinori Kaya; the navy minister, Shigetaro Shimada; the foreign minister, Shigenori Togo; and the minister without portfolio, Teiichi Suzuki. The remaining seven were Naoki Hoshino, the chief cabinet secretary; General Heitaro Kimura, the vice minister of war; General Akira Muto, the chief of the war ministry's military affairs bureau; General Kenryo Sato, a section chief under Muto; Admiral Osumi Nagano, the navy chief of staff; Admiral Takasumi Oka, chief of the navy ministry's general and military affairs bureau; and Marquis Kido, Lord Keeper of the Privy Seal.

The list of defendants also included three former prime ministers in addition to Tojo. Baron Kiichiro Hiranuma had served briefly during 1938. Baron Koki Hirota, prime minister from March 1936 to February 1937, was also a former foreign minister. General Kuniaki Koiso was prime minister from July 1944, after Tojo resigned in disgrace because the war was going badly, to April 1945.

Six defendants were diplomats. Two in addition to Hirota and Togo were former foreign ministers. They were Yosuke Matsuoka, Japan's foreign minister from July 1940 to July 1941, and Mamoru Shigemitsu. Shigemitsu, a career diplomat and former ambassador, was foreign minister in the Tojo and Koiso cabinets from April 1943 to April 1945. He also served briefly as foreign minister after Japan's surrender. While holding that

Tojo (second from right) and the other defendants at lunch during the trial.

postwar office, Shigemitsu had the dubious honor of signing the surrender papers in September 1945. Two defendants in addition to Shigemitsu were former ambassadors. They were General Hiroshi Oshima, Japan's wartime ambassador to Germany, and Toshio Shiratori, ambassador to Italy from 1938 to 1940.

Seven defendants in addition to those mentioned above were military officials. Four were former war ministers: General Sadao Araki (1931–1934), General

Seishiro Itagaki (1938–1939), General Jiro Minami (1931), and Field Marshal Shunroku Hata (1939–1940). All except Araki had also held field commands. There were also three other generals who had commanded Japanese armies: Kenji Doihara, Iwane Matsui, and Yoshijiro Umezu, the last wartime army chief of staff, who signed the surrender papers on behalf of the Japanese armed forces.

There were two defendants who didn't seem to fit the description of major war criminals. One, Shumei Okawa, had never held a major public office. However, this radical Japanese nationalist had been a rabid supporter of Japanese wars in Asia. He had also been involved in three plots against Japanese cabinets that opposed the warmongers in the Japanese Army. He was included in the list of defendants because of these activities. The other defendant, Colonel Kingoro Hashimoto, had never achieved top military rank. However, he had played leading roles in both the 1931 Mukden incident and the plots against Japanese governments during the 1930s. In addition (and perhaps most important from the American viewpoint), Hashimoto ordered the attack on the American gunboat *Panay* in 1937.

There was one notable omission from the list of defendants. It was Emperor Hirohito, who was regarded by many Americans as the principal war criminal. During the war years, Americans (still smarting over the insult of Pearl Harbor) had trouble deciding which Japanese leader they hated most, Tojo or Hirohito.

Although many Americans wanted to see Hirohito tried and punished as a war criminal, a number of government officials, particularly the State Department specialists on Japan, saw things differently. These officials believed that Hirohito's power was largely symbolic, and that the real power lay with the prime ministers and other top cabinet officials, whose advice the Emperor was expected to follow. Moreover, in their opinion, keeping Hirohito on the Japanese throne would prevent postwar anarchy or a Communist takeover of Japan. Eventually, President Harry S. Truman was convinced of the wisdom of allowing Hirohito to stay on as emperor. Once the Americans made their decision, they persuaded the other Allies to go along. (The British, who had never wanted to try Hirohito, didn't need much persuasion.)

While one group of prosecutors was selecting the defendants, another group headed by the British prosecutor, Arthur S. Comyns-Carr, worked on the preparation of the indictment. Instead of only four counts, as at Nuremberg, the indictment of the Japanese contained fifty-five separate counts, divided into three main groups: (1) crimes against peace, (2) murder, and (3) conventional war crimes and crimes against humanity.

There were thirty-six counts of crimes against peace. Count 1, the basic charge, accused all the defendants of participating in a conspiracy, beginning in 1928, to secure the military, naval, political, and economic domination of East Asia and the entire region in and around the Pacific and Indian oceans. Counts 2 through 36 divided the charge of crimes against peace into more specific charges.

There were sixteen counts of murder. Counts 37 and 38 charged some defendants with conspiracies to kill soldiers and civilians in certain countries by starting unlawful wars. Counts 39 through 52 covered specific instances of murder or conspiracies to murder.

There were three counts of conventional war crimes and crimes against humanity. Count 53 charged some defendants with conspiring to order or permit Japanese atrocities against Allied soldiers and civilians. Count 54

Emperor Hirohito signs Japan's new
constitution in this official photograph,
taken in 1946. The decision not to bring
charges against him was controversial.

charged some with actually ordering or permitting atrocities. Count 55 charged some with recklessly disregarding their duty to prevent atrocities.

This last charge was a departure from the Nuremberg indictment. None of the defendants at Nuremberg had been charged with a crime because of their failure to do something. Count 55 bore the earmarks of an American addition to the indictment. Shortly after the war ended, American military commissions tried two Japanese generals on "reckless disregard" charges. (See Chapter Eight for a discussion of these trials.) Count 55 would be a source of continuing controversy over the years.

In February 1946, MacArthur appointed eleven judges for the IMTFE, one from each ally in the Pacific war. Meanwhile, a host of Japanese and American workers were converting the auditorium of the Japanese war ministry headquarters to a courtroom suitable for an important trial. The war ministry building was one of the few in Tokyo that hadn't been damaged by bombs. Also, as at Nuremberg, the site had an appealing symbolism. It seemed fitting that the Japanese militarists should face judgment in the place where they had planned their wars of aggression.

The prosecutors presented the indictments to the IMTFE on April 29, 1946. Copies were given to the defendants, and the tribunal's first session was set for May 3, 1946. The stage was set for the Japanese counterpart to Nuremberg.

Chapter Seven

TOKYO
—
THE INTERNATIONAL MILITARY TRIBUNAL

The auditorium of the Japanese war ministry's headquarters was crowded on the morning of May 3, 1946,
as the defendants, escorted by white-gloved and white-
helmeted American military police, shuffled into the
makeshift courtroom for the start of their trial. Sir William Flood Webb of Australia, the president of the International Military Tribunal for the Far East, announced somewhat pompously during his opening
statement that there had been no more important trial in
all history than the one about to begin. *Time* magazine
remarked a couple of weeks later, however, that the
Tokyo trial looked like a third-string road-company version of the Nuremberg show.[5]

The trial lasted almost two years. During that time,
the judges heard the testimony of more than 400 witnesses and received written statements from about 800
others. Over 4,000 documents were submitted as evidence. The official record was almost 80,000 pages
long. After the trial ended, the judges took almost seven

**IMTFE defendants. Front row, from left:
Doihara, Hata, Hirota, Minami, Tojo, Oka, Umezu,
Araki, Muto, Hoshino, Kaya, Kido. Second row:
Hashimoto, Koiso, Nagano, Oshima, Matsui,
Okawa, Hiranuma, Togo, Matsuoka, Shigemitsu,
Sato, Shimada, Shiratori, Suzuki. Itagaki and
Kimura are not shown.**

months to reach their decisions. The reading of the 207 separate verdicts and 25 individual sentences took eight days. The court finally adjourned on November 12, 1948, a little more than two and a half years after its first session.

As at Nuremberg, nothing in the defendants' appearance during the opening session suggested that this group of aging men had once held vast power. All were over fifty. Three were over seventy. The oldest, the glum, horse-faced Baron Hiranuma, was almost eighty. Many of the defendants were in poor health; two died before the trial ended. Matsuoka, whose painfully slow steps, pale face, and sunken cheeks showed how close to death he was at the opening session, died from tuberculosis on June 27, 1946. Admiral Nagano died from the disease on January 5, 1947.

During the opening session, in a scene that smacked of low comedy, Okawa interrupted the reading of the indictment by whacking Tojo's bald head. American military police hustled Okawa out of the courtroom while he babbled that he had to kill Tojo, then declared that the United States was "democrazy." Shortly afterward, a group of doctors examined Okawa and pronounced him unfit to stand trial. He was kept in a mental hospital throughout the trial and released at the end of 1948. By that time the charges against him had been dropped. Many suspected that Okawa, who conveniently recovered once he no longer faced criminal charges, had been sane all along.

Several of the judges were a source of controversy. Some defense lawyers challenged the appointment of two judges on the grounds that they couldn't give unbiased verdicts. One judge was Delfin Jaranilla of the Philippine Supreme Court, who had survived the Bataan Death March. The other was the tribunal president,

Webb, who had investigated Japanese atrocities in New Guinea during the war. The tribunal voted to allow both judges to remain.

Early in July 1946, the American member of the tribunal, Judge John P. Higgins of the Massachusetts Superior Court, resigned. MacArthur then appointed Army Judge Advocate General Myron C. Cramer to replace Higgins. This move was controversial. Some thought Higgins's slot should remain vacant because MacArthur had no authority to name a replacement. (The IMTFE charter authorized him to name up to eleven judges. Cramer was the twelfth judge to be named.) Others believed that the tribunal must include an American judge. When Cramer arrived in Tokyo toward the end of July, several defense attorneys called for a mistrial on the grounds that Cramer had missed part of the testimony and thus couldn't give a fair verdict. Because the charter of the Tokyo tribunal allowed judges who missed part of the trial to take part in subsequent proceedings unless they disqualified themselves, the tribunal decided to allow the trial to proceed. However, absences of individual judges continued to be a problem as the trial dragged on.

The associate counsels for the prosecution were all experienced lawyers or judges. The French and Dutch prosecutors both had previous experience with the trial of war criminals. Most of the prosecutors seemed well suited by temperament as well as experience to argue such a politically sensitive case. The American chief counsel, Keenan, was an exception, however. Keenan was an outspoken man whose red nose seemed to justify his reputation for hard drinking. His appearance added to the circus atmosphere of the Tokyo trial. (Keenan bore a striking resemblance to the popular American comedian W. C. Fields.) The American prosecutor also

William Webb of Australia (center) was president of the Tokyo tribunal. U.S. judge John P. Higgins, to Webb's right in this picture, resigned soon after the trial began.

had a habit of using extravagant language in court. His courtroom antics annoyed both his fellow prosecutors (at one point, some of Keenan's American assistants asked MacArthur to fire him) and the tribunal president. Webb, a quick-tempered, tactless man, often clashed with Keenan during the trial.

Both Japanese and American lawyers represented the defendants. The Japanese government had asked for American defense lawyers because most Japanese lawyers were unfamiliar with Anglo-American trial procedures. The American lawyers had a difficult job on their hands. Although the Japanese lawyers were generally well qualified, the language barrier was a serious problem. (It is very hard to translate Japanese into other languages.) Most of the Americans could neither speak nor understand Japanese, and many of the Japanese defendants couldn't speak English. Defending some of the accused men would have been hard enough under the best conditions. Defendants such as Tojo seemed sure to be convicted. (Tojo himself recognized this. At one point he told his American lawyer, "I know they are going to hang me.") Despite the many obstacles they faced, the defense attorneys worked hard to defend their clients. Some of the American lawyers showed a surprising zeal in defending men who had been at war with them only a short time earlier.

The prosecution took a little more than seven months to present its case. The prosecutors divided it into fourteen separate phases. The first phase gave a short history of Japan from 1928 to 1945, an explanation of the structure and operation of the Japanese government, and a summary of the defendants' official positions during that period. The second phase showed how a group of militarists gained control of the Japanese government during the 1930s and subsequently fed their

Chief prosecutor Joseph B. Keenan opens the Allied case. Taking notes in the foreground is Ichiro Kiyose, chief Japanese defense counsel, who personally handled Tojo's defense.

militaristic propaganda to the Japanese people while Japan prepared for war. The prosecutors felt that these preliminary explanations were necessary for an understanding of Japan's decision to make war on its neighbors and the Western powers.

The prosecution then cited specific instances of Japanese war crimes. The list was long: Japan's takeover of Manchuria, its attacks on the rest of China, its use of the illegal opium traffic in China as a way both of controlling the Chinese and of financing the Japanese-controlled governments, its experiments in germ warfare, its alliance with Germany and Italy in an effort to achieve world domination, its mobilization of the Japanese economy in preparation for war, and its aggressive wars in Southeast Asia and the Pacific islands. (The prosecution devoted more than a month to the presentation of evidence regarding Japan's surprise attack on Pearl Harbor, an act that still angered the Americans.) Finally, the prosecution presented evidence tying individual defendants to one or more war crimes.

The prosecution introduced many official Japanese documents as evidence, plus one important unofficial document. Shortly after his arrest, Kido gave his captors a diary he had kept both before and during the war. The diary, which described the emperor's and Kido's attempts to rein in the warmongers, provided incriminating evidence against several defendants, including Kido himself. In what he described as an effort to "guide" the militarists, Kido had recommended the appointment of Tojo as prime minister in October 1941.

The prosecution's evidence included a seemingly endless parade of testimony on Japanese wartime atrocities. Some of the evidence was weak, but much of it came from the mouths of reliable eyewitnesses, who told chilling tales of mass rape, torture, and murder by Japanese troops, the dreadful conditions endured by prisoners of war, and the use of both civilians and war prisoners as slave labor. There was testimony about the Rape of Nanking, the mistreatment of the slave workers who helped to build the Siam-Burma railroad during 1942 and 1943 (the so-called Death Railway), and the abysmal conditions on the "hellships" used to transport these workers. Fourteen thousand pages of affidavits described Japanese atrocities in the Philippines. Many of the defendants bowed their heads or closed their eyes during this type of testimony. Some were hearing the stories for the first time. Others felt the hangman's noose tighten with each new recital.

Many of those who attended the trial had a hard time reconciling the stories of the brutality of Japanese troops with the behavior of Japanese civilians, who seemed friendly and polite. As at Nuremberg, the tribunal made it clear that the men in the courtroom, not the Japanese people, were on trial. Some people felt, however, that the Japanese people, like the German people, shared their leaders' guilt. Present-day Japan is still trying to deal with Japanese wartime atrocities. And even though the prosecution tried hard to keep him out of the picture, Emperor Hirohito was on trial in a real sense. Many people regarded him as a living symbol of Japanese aggression. Even today, historians differ on the question of Hirohito's war guilt.

The defense opened its case on February 24, 1947. Defense attorneys had already unsuccessfully challenged the tribunal on several issues, using some of the same arguments that had been made at Nuremberg—notably, that aggressive war wasn't a crime under international law, and that a court consisting only of representatives of the winning side couldn't be fair. Now they began with a joint defense against the prosecution's main charges, then moved to the individual defenses.

During the general presentation, the lawyers argued that no criminal conspiracy had taken place. They pointed to the many different cabinets with different officials that had existed in Japan during the 1930s and 1940s and noted that the defendants often disagreed among themselves. These factors argued against the notion of a unified band of conspirators pursuing a long-range common goal. The defense lawyers argued further that all of Japan's actions were taken either in defense against the threatening acts of other countries or in a legitimate effort to protect Japanese interests. They also contended that the poor treatment of war prisoners and enemy civilians resulted from the Allied military actions, which destroyed much of Japan's ability to provide food and medical care for both enemy nationals and its own people.

The defense also tried to introduce evidence that some of the countries sitting in judgment against Japan were themselves guilty of war crimes. The tribunal refused to allow this evidence, but many people felt that the defense had a point. As at Nuremberg, nobody's hands were entirely clean. The British, French, and Dutch colonies in Asia, then struggling for independence, were ample evidence of Western imperialism. Moreover, many both at the time and in later years regarded the American fire-bombings of Tokyo and the atomic bombings of Hiroshima and Nagasaki, which killed thousands of Japanese civilians, as war crimes.

In November 1947, while the individual defenses were in progress, Webb, who was a justice on the Australian High Court, went back to Australia for that court's fall session. During his absence, nine individual defendants presented their cases. Webb's absence during this period provoked an angry outburst from one defense attorney, who accused the judges of abusing their privilege of missing some trial sessions.

It is questionable whether Webb's absence affected his decisions regarding the individual defendants. Most of the individual defenses were not strong. Defense witnesses often contradicted themselves during their testimony, and some of their evidence actually supported the prosecution rather than the defense. Moreover, some of the defense witnesses were themselves suspected war criminals. The defendants tended to blame one another for what happened. The civilian officials argued that they were powerless against the military leaders. The war ministers and military staff officers claimed that the field commanders were responsible for the care of prisoners and enemy civilians, and the field commanders claimed that they were simply following orders.

Tojo, however, refused to blame others for his predicament. Unrepentant, he accepted full responsibility for all of his acts, which he claimed were unavoidable and without evil intent. Tojo's testimony, delivered before a packed auditorium, was one of the highlights of a trial often dominated by boredom. Keenan cross-examined Tojo himself, even though he had not prepared the case against the former Japanese prime minister. Keenan's clumsy cross-examination reminded some observers of Justice Jackson's uncertain performance in cross-examining Hermann Goering during the Nuremberg trial. At one point Keenan blundered into getting Tojo to admit that no Japanese would dare to act against the emperor's will. This seeming admission of Hirohito's war guilt resulted in a frantic behind-the-scenes scramble to get Tojo to "clarify" his statement. Tojo later absolved the emperor of responsibility for starting the war.

The defense closed its case on January 12, 1948. The tribunal then announced its decision to accept new evidence from the prosecution. The defense, after objecting in vain that the prosecution had already closed its case, insisted on its right to respond to the new evidence. (At that point it seemed as if the trial would never end!) After the prosecution's further evidence and the defense response, the tribunal adjourned on April 6, 1948, almost two years after the opening sessions, to consider its verdicts.

A seven-member committee of judges drafted the tribunal's judgment, which were written without discussion by the full tribunal. (The IMTFE's charter required

Tojo takes the stand in one of the
trial's most dramatic moments.

only that all decisions be the result of a majority vote. The drafting committee had one more member than the required majority of six judges.) Although he had served as president of the tribunal, Webb was not on the committee, which consisted of judges from the United States (with Cramer as chair), Great Britain, China, the Soviet Union, Canada, New Zealand, and the Philippines.

When the tribunal met on November 4, 1948, to announce its judgments, three defendants—Shiratori, Umezu, and Hiranuma—were too sick to attend the session. Hiranuma later recovered enough to come to court. Kaya also missed some of the final sessions because of illness.

The judges dismissed all but ten of the fifty-five counts for various reasons. They found all defendants guilty of taking part in a conspiracy to wage aggressive war except Matsui and Shigemitsu, who had spent most of the prewar period outside Japan. The judges also found all defendants except Matsui, Oshima, and Shiratori guilty of waging aggressive war against one or more countries. Oshima and Shiratori, both diplomats, had nothing to do with the actual waging of the war, although both were convicted of conspiracy because of their efforts in negotiating Japan's wartime alliance with Germany and Italy (the so-called Rome-Berlin-Tokyo Axis). Matsui was also acquitted of all charges of waging aggressive war, even though he was commander in chief of the Japanese forces in central China for a brief period in late 1937 and early 1938.

In reaching its decisions regarding conventional war crimes and crimes against humanity, the court found that Japanese atrocities were so widespread, yet followed so common a pattern, that only one conclusion was possible: The atrocities were either ordered or permitted by the Japanese government and the leaders of the Japanese armed forces. The court noted that both military commanders and civil government officials, particularly cabinet members, have a continuing responsibility to see that enemy soldiers and civilians are not mistreated. Those who order or permit such mistreatment, and those who know about it (or willfully neglect to learn about it) and fail to take adequate steps to prevent its recurrence are as guilty as those who actually commit the atrocities.

Based on these general principles, the court found five defendants guilty of ordering or permitting atrocities (Count 54). Four—Doihara, Itagaki, Kimura, and Muto—were field commanders whose troops committed large numbers of atrocities. These four generals were also responsible for the operation of prisoner-of-war camps where inmates were mistreated. Tojo, a former field commander who ordered the use of prisoners of war as slave labor while he was prime minister, was also convicted under Count 54.

Seven defendants were convicted of recklessly disregarding their duty to prevent atrocities (Count 55). They were Hata, Kimura, Koiso, Matsui, Muto, Hirota, and Shigemitsu. The first five had all commanded Japanese armies in the field and thus were responsible for the acts of their troops. Koiso was also a wartime prime minister with overall responsibility for Japan's conduct of the war. As foreign ministers, both Hirota and Shigemitsu knew about some of the Japanese atrocities through the protests of foreign diplomats in Tokyo, although it wasn't clear what they could have done to stop these crimes. Togo, who also served briefly as Japan's foreign minister, was acquitted of the charges under both Counts 54 and 55, as was Umezu, a former field commander and army chief of staff.

After the tribunal announced its verdicts, the defendants, all of whom were convicted of at least one crime, were brought into the courtroom one by one to hear their sentences. The sentencing took only seventeen minutes, an average of less than one minute per defendant. The sentences ranged from death to seven years in prison. Seven defendants (Doihara, Hirota, Itagaki, Kimura, Matsui, Muto, and Tojo) were sentenced to hang. Togo received a twenty-year sentence and Shigemitsu a seven-year sentence. The others were sentenced to life imprisonment.

Most people expected Tojo and the five generals to hang. The sentences seemed inconsistent on the whole, however. For example, Hirota and Matsui were sentenced to death even though they were found innocent of actually ordering any atrocities. Oshima, convicted only of conspiracy, received a life sentence, while Togo, convicted of both conspiracy and waging aggressive war, received only twenty years, and Shigemitsu, convicted of waging aggressive war and recklessly disregarding his duty to prevent atrocities, received the lightest sentence of all, seven years. (Togo and Shigemitsu may have received lesser sentences than the other defendants because of evidence showing that they joined Tojo's cabinet in the hope of working for peace.)

The tribunal's decisions were not unanimous. Three judges filed dissenting opinions, and two filed separate concurring opinions. These opinions were not read in court. Webb simply mentioned their existence during his reading of the judgment. They were made part of the official record, however.

Judge Henri Bernard of France objected to the failure to indict Hirohito. He also said that defects of procedure, such as the failure of the whole tribunal to discuss the proposed findings and the trying of the defendants as a group instead of as individuals, made the verdicts invalid.

Judge Bernard Röling of the Netherlands believed that Oka, Sato, and Shimada should have been convicted of conventional war crimes and sentenced to death, while Hata, Hirota, Kido, Shigemitsu, and Togo should have been acquitted of all charges. Röling also disagreed with the court's reasoning regarding the charge of failing to prevent atrocities (Count 55). He believed that knowledge of war crimes wasn't enough for a conviction under this count. The convicted person must also have had both a direct responsibility for the treatment of enemy soldiers and civilians and the power to prevent their mistreatment.

Judge Radhabinod Pal of India wrote a 1,200-page dissent in which he argued that all defendants should have been acquitted. Pal believed that waging aggressive war was not a crime under international law, and that it was unfair to punish Japan for acts that didn't differ materially from the past actions of the Western powers in achieving dominance in Asia. (Pal may have been influenced by India's experience as a British colony. After a long struggle, India became independent in August 1947.) Pal also believed that reckless disregard of duty, which was not mentioned as a crime in the IMTFE's charter, was outside its jurisdiction.

In his concurring opinion, Webb, who believed that Hirohito should have been tried for war crimes, said that the emperor's immunity from prosecution should have been considered in imposing the sentences. He believed that those who were sentenced to death should have received life sentences instead. Jaranilla, on the other hand, believed that some sentences were too lenient, although he concurred in the judgments.

Many agreed with Judge Röling's opinion regarding Hirota. They thought the sentence was too harsh because Hirota, the only civilian to receive the death penalty, wasn't in a position to stop the atrocities committed by Japanese troops in other countries. Hirota's lawyers may have foreseen the trial's outcome for their client. They had asked that Hirota be tried separately, claiming that trying him with the military defendants made it impossible for him to receive a fair trial.

After the judgments were announced, the defense lawyers appealed to MacArthur, claiming that their clients hadn't received a fair trial. MacArthur had the authority to reduce the sentences, but first he had to consult the diplomatic representatives of the eleven Allies in the Pacific war. The meeting, which lasted only a half hour, took place on November 24, 1948. MacArthur's political adviser, William J. Sebald, led off by saying that he had no changes to recommend. The representatives of the six other Allies whose judges were on the drafting committee also recommended no changes, although the Canadian diplomat said he wouldn't object to any reductions in the sentences. The Australian diplomat made a similar statement, while the French diplomat urged MacArthur to consider clemency. The Indian diplomat favored commuting all death sentences to life imprisonment. The diplomat from the Netherlands recommended the commutation of Hirota's sentence to life imprisonment and the reduction of Hata's, Umezu's, Togo's, and Shigemitsu's sentences. Despite these statements, MacArthur upheld all the sentences, saying he found nothing in the trial sufficiently important to warrant his intervention in its judgments.

Some defendants then appealed to the U.S. Supreme Court, claiming that MacArthur had no authority to set up the tribunal. The Court agreed to hear arguments on the case, but after the Far Eastern Commission declared that the tribunal was an international court, appointed and operating under international authority, the Court decided on December 20, 1948, that it had no authority to review the sentences.

The seven condemned men were hanged at Sugamo Prison shortly after midnight on December 23, 1948. Five of the convicted men died while serving their prison terms: Shiratori and Umezu in 1949, Koiso and Togo in 1950, and Hiranuma in 1952. Shigemitsu was released on parole in 1950, and the others were paroled in the mid-1950s. By that time the peace treaty had been signed and Japan, once a bitter enemy, was a staunch ally in the Cold War against the Communist nations.

The Tokyo trial was controversial both at the time and in later years. Some defendants may have been convicted unfairly, and some sentences seemed inconsistent. The trial itself was marred by its excessive length and by the frequent unseemly wrangling among judges, prosecutors, and defense attorneys that contributed to the circus atmosphere that many observers noted. In retrospect, *Time*'s 1946 description of the Tokyo trial as a third-string road-company show may not have been far off the mark. Still, that trial, like its Nuremberg counterpart, provided a permanent record of the brutal and savage crimes that shocked the world more than half a century ago.

Chapter Eight

OTHER WAR CRIMES TRIALS IN THE FAR EAST

The twenty-five defendants convicted of war crimes by the international tribunal in Tokyo represented only a small fraction of the suspected Japanese war criminals. By the end of 1945, occupation officials had identified more than 2,500 suspects, of whom about 600 had already been charged with war crimes. If the Allies hoped to bring the bulk of the war criminals to justice, many trials would be necessary.[6]

The Americans began to hold war crimes trials not long after Japan's surrender. From the fall of 1945 until October 1949, when the last American trial ended, the United States conducted almost 500 trials involving over 1,400 defendants at various locations in Asia and the Pacific islands. In addition, the United States cooperated with other Allies in the prosecution of Japanese who committed atrocities against Americans.

The earliest American trials took place in Manila. As American troops regained control over most of the Philippines during the spring of 1945, investigators began collecting evidence of war crimes. By the time Japan surrendered, there was enough evidence to justify charging a number of Japanese with war crimes in the Philippines. The first to be tried was General Tomoyuki Yamashita, who commanded the Japanese Fourteenth Area Army in the Philippines from October 1944 until the end of the war. The Yamashita trial proved to be one of the most controversial trials of the postwar period.

MacArthur had a personal interest in the punishment of those who had committed war crimes in the Philippines. He had spent a good part of his military career there, both before and during the Pacific war. MacArthur commanded the U.S. armed forces in the Philippines at the time of the Japanese air attack in December 1941. He retained the Philippine command until March 1942, when President Roosevelt ordered him to go to Australia to take command of the Allied forces in the southwest Pacific. MacArthur returned to the Philippines in October 1944 to lead the campaign to free the islands from Japanese rule.

The Philippine campaign was bitter and bloody. When the Americans entered Manila in March 1945, they found a devastated city and evidence that the Japanese had massacred thousands of Filipino civilians. By that time, Yamashita had retreated with most of his troops to the mountains of northern Luzon (the island on which Manila is located). Cut off by the Americans from communication with other Japanese forces, Yamashita held out in his mountain headquarters until he learned of Japan's surrender.

The main charge against Yamashita, put into the indictment at MacArthur's request, was Yamashita's failure to keep his troops from committing atrocities during the Allied campaign to retake the Philippines. Military laws had long recognized that a commanding officer

Tomoyuki Yamashita, former commander of Japanese forces in the Philippines, in custody.

was responsible for the actions of those under his command. This rule is called command responsibility. The rule had always assumed, however, that the commander knew what his troops were doing and was in a position to control their actions. There was no evidence that Yamashita personally ordered any atrocities, or that he even knew about those that occurred in Manila in February 1945. There was also room for doubt about the extent of Yamashita's authority over Japanese forces in the Philippines.

MacArthur was clearly breaking new ground in charging Yamashita with unlawfully disregarding his duty to control those under his command—the charge that became Count 55 in the Tokyo trial. SCAP officials asked the War Department for a legal opinion to support this charge, but on September 24, 1945, MacArthur ordered Lieutenant General Wilhelm Styer, the commander of the American army in the western Pacific, to proceed with Yamashita's trial without waiting for the War Department's reply.

Yamashita's trial took place in Manila before a U.S. military commission consisting of five judges, all career officers under General Styer's command. During the trial, which began in late October 1945 and lasted about a month, the prosecutors used the same tactics that were later used in the Tokyo trial. The prosecution produced a parade of witnesses who told graphic and emotional tales of torture, rape, and murder by Japanese troops throughout the Philippines, then argued that these atrocities were so widespread, repeated, and notorious that Yamashita must either have known about them or taken care to see that he didn't know. The six defense attorneys, who were also army officers under General Styer's command, first tried to challenge the court's jurisdiction. When that failed to work, the defense produced evidence about the difficulties that Yamashita experienced under battle conditions: inexperienced and poorly disciplined troops, lack of food and other supplies, and lack of communication between Yamashita's troops in northern Luzon and those scattered over other parts of the island.

The defense also pointed out the problems that Yamashita faced because of a division of Japanese military authority in the Philippines. Japanese naval forces in Manila had committed most of the atrocities in that city. The sailors, although technically under Yamashita's command while on shore, were ordinarily under the command of Vice Admiral Denshishi Okochi, head of the Southwest Area Fleet, and Okochi's superior officer, Admiral Soemu Toyoda, head of the Combined Pacific Fleet. As the Allies advanced on Manila, Yamashita ordered the naval forces to withdraw from the city, but the sailors, having received conflicting orders from the navy, ignored Yamashita's order.

Yamashita himself testified that he had never ordered any of the atrocities and that he had done his best to control his troops under extremely difficult conditions. Yamashita made a very impressive showing during his testimony, but it did him no good. On December 7, 1945, the judges found Yamashita guilty and sentenced him to hang. The judges accepted the prosecution's reasoning in reaching their verdict, stating: "The crimes were so extensive and widespread that they must either have been willfully permitted . . . or secretly ordered by the accused."

After an unsuccessful appeal to the Philippine Supreme Court, the defense appealed to the U.S. Supreme Court, which agreed to consider the case. The Court confined itself to the narrow question of whether the military commission had the authority to try Yamashita.

Having concluded that the military commission was lawfully established, the Court held in February 1946 that it lacked the authority to review the commission's decision. In the Court's opinion, the military authorities alone had such power.

Two justices, Wiley Rutledge and Frank Murphy, disagreed with the majority and filed dissenting opinions. Justice Murphy's dissent was especially critical of the military commission's decision to convict Yamashita of failing to control his troops. Murphy pointed out that American forces had succeeded in destroying Yamashita's lines of communication and control of his personnel. Then, after Yamashita's disorganized troops committed widespread atrocities, the Americans charged him with failure to control them. Murphy then stated, "To use the very inefficiency and disorganization created by the victorious forces as the primary basis for condemning officers of the defeated armies bears no resemblance to justice or military reality." (Murphy may have been at least partly motivated by dislike for MacArthur. Murphy, who had been U.S. high commissioner in the Philippines during the 1930s, often tangled with MacArthur during that period.) After learning of the Supreme Court's decision, MacArthur upheld Yamashita's death sentence. Yamashita was hanged in Manila on February 23, 1946.

Late in December 1945, an American military commission in Manila tried another Japanese general, Masaharu Homma, for war crimes that took place from December 1941 to August 1942, while Homma commanded Japanese troops in the Philippines. The charges against Homma included responsibility for Japanese atrocities during the Death March on Bataan Peninsula after the Americans surrendered to the Japanese in April 1942 and the abuse of prisoners of war in Philippine prison camps. As in Yamashita's case, there was no evidence that Homma had ordered any of these atrocities, although he may have known about some of them. Homma's trial followed the pattern set in the Yamashita case: prosecution testimony regarding atrocities; defense pleas concerning the difficulties that Homma faced under battle conditions; a guilty verdict and death sentence; an appeal to the U.S. Supreme Court; a denial of the appeal, with Justices Rutledge and Murphy again dissenting; and MacArthur's upholding of the sentence. Only the punishment differed; Homma was executed by a firing squad in April 1946.

While the Yamashita and Homma trials were going on, the Americans reached an agreement with the Chinese government to try Japanese accused of war crimes against Americans in China. There were eleven such trials involving seventy-five defendants beginning in January 1946. In addition, the U.S. Navy held almost fifty trials involving more than a hundred defendants on various Pacific islands. Most of the Navy trials involved the murder of Americans on islands captured by the Japanese during the war.

By far the greatest number of American war crimes trials took place in Yokohama, Japan, where U.S. Army tribunals tried almost a thousand defendants in more than three hundred separate trials. (Although American officials conducted these trials, they were considered international trials because they were held under SCAP's authority as an Allied occupation force.) The defendants at Yokohama included generals and admirals, lower-ranking military personnel, and civilians engaged in a variety of occupations.[7]

The Americans at Yokohama followed the practice of their counterparts in Germany by dividing the cases into different categories of crimes and trying the defendants in groups to speed and simplify the trials. The Yokohama trials fell into seven categories: (1) prisoner-of-war command responsibility cases; (2) prisoner-of-war camp cases; (3) airmen atrocities; (4) denial of fair trials; (5) ceremonial murders; (6) acts of revenge; and (7) medical experiments on prisoners of war. The first two categories involved Japanese officials accused of failing to carry out their duty to see that war prisoners were treated humanely, ordering the mistreatment of prisoners, or actually mistreating them. The third and fourth categories dealt with the mistreatment or execution of American fliers captured in Japan. The fifth and sixth categories involved the execution of captured Americans either as part of ancient Japanese military rituals or in revenge for Japanese battle casualties. The last category involved Japanese doctors, nurses, and scientists who carried out cruel experiments on American prisoners of war.

By the time the Tokyo tribunal announced its judgments in November 1948, the Americans were trying to end the war crimes trials in both Germany and the Far East. In August 1947, SCAP freed fifteen Class A suspects from Sugamo Prison, saying that the evidence against them wasn't strong enough to justify putting them on trial. Other Class A suspects were released in February 1948. On December 24, 1948, after the death sentences imposed by the Tokyo tribunal were carried out, SCAP released nineteen remaining Class A suspects, saying, "This release completes the disposition of all former major war crimes suspects held in Japan."

In October 1948, SCAP charged two Japanese originally held as Class A suspects with Class B and C war crimes. One was Admiral Soemu Toyoda, who had commanded the Combined Japanese Pacific Fleet at the time of the Rape of Manila. In September 1949, after a lengthy trial, Toyoda was acquitted of responsibility for war crimes committed by Japanese naval personnel under his command. Toyoda's acquittal showed how American attitudes toward Japan had changed in the four years following Japan's surrender. General Yamashita, tried soon after the war ended, was hanged for failing to prevent Japanese atrocities, while Admiral Toyoda, charged three years later with similar offenses, endured less than four years of confinement.

The move to free convicted Japanese war criminals began almost as soon as the last trial ended in October 1949. Early in 1950, SCAP established a parole board with authority to release prisoners who had served at least one third of their sentences. The Soviets complained about the establishment of the parole board, but SCAP ignored their complaints. By that time the wartime alliance with the Soviet Union had completely fallen apart.

In September 1952, following the signing of the peace treaty with Japan in April of that year, President Harry S. Truman replaced SCAP's parole board with an American clemency and parole board composed of representatives of the State, Defense, and Justice departments. In January 1958, President Dwight D. Eisenhower abolished this board and agreed to accept the Japanese government's recommendations regarding the release of convicted war criminals. In April 1958, the Allies agreed to the unconditional release of the ten surviving men convicted by the Tokyo tribunal, all of whom had been paroled a few years earlier. On December 31, 1958, the United States announced the release of eighty-three convicted war criminals from Sugamo Prison. The freeing of these last remaining prisoners officially ended the American effort to punish Japanese war criminals.

EPILOGUE

After the international military tribunal at Nuremberg reached its judgments, two members of the American prosecution staff analyzed the trial's results for the readers of *The New Republic*. In an October 1946 article, Thomas L. Karsten and James H. Mathias wrote:

> First and foremost, a great moral principle has been judicially established—the principle that the planning and waging of aggressive war is the greatest crime known to mankind and that those guilty of perpetrating it shall be punished. Hardly less important than the principle itself is the recognition . . . that national sovereignty is no longer a shield behind which aggressors may take refuge.

Karsten and Mathias then cautioned their readers that the establishment of this moral principle didn't mean that no nation would ever again wage a war of aggression. Although they believed that the principle could act as an inhibiting force, it wasn't enough in itself to deter aggression. They added:

> The principle must be implemented by the nations of the world acting in concert under the aegis of a strong international organization having adequate powers to deal with potential aggressors. Unless this is done the advances made at Nuremberg will be illusory and mankind may again stand on the brink of self-destruction.[8]

When Karsten and Mathias wrote the magazine article, the weakness of the recently formed United Nations as a peacekeeper was already apparent. The United Nations had no army, navy, or police force and no permanent international court with the authority to punish international criminals. Moreover, any of the five permanent members of the UN Security Council (the United States, Great Britain, France, China, and the Soviet Union) could stop the council from issuing an order simply by voting against it. This right, known as the veto power, was included in the UN Charter because of fears that the world body might interfere in a country's internal affairs. National sovereignty was still extremely important to the victorious Allies.

In spite of its weakness, the United Nations has had some success as a peacekeeper. In the half-century since the end of World War II, no new world war has broken out, and some international disputes have been settled peaceably. There have been numerous local conflicts, however, as old empires have disintegrated and new nations have struggled to emerge from the ruins. Ancient ethnic, religious, and national enmities have periodically flared up into open warfare in different parts of the world. The United States alone has engaged in two lengthy wars in Asia and several shorter conflicts in other localities.

Both of the Asian conflicts were attempts to prevent Communist expansion in Asia. The Korean War, which started in 1950 in response to Communist North Korea's invasion of South Korea, was conducted under the authority of the UN. Although the war wasn't an unqualified military success, it prevented a Communist takeover of South Korea. On the other hand, the Vietnam War, which began in the mid-1960s as an American attempt to protect South Vietnam from its Communist neighbor, North Vietnam, ended in what many saw as a humiliating American defeat. In 1975, after the American forces had left Vietnam, the former French colony was reunited under Communist rule.

The American experience in Vietnam forced Americans to consider the issue of war crimes from another perspective. This time it was the Americans who were branded as war criminals. American outrage over North Vietnam's threat to try captured fliers who bombed North Vietnamese cities as war criminals (a threat that was never carried out) became mixed with shame over scattered reports of atrocities that American ground troops committed against Vietnamese civilians. The shame and anger grew after Americans learned that a platoon of U.S. soldiers had rampaged through the South Vietnamese village of My Lai in March 1968, slaughtering its residents, including infants and small children. Americans were ashamed of the atrocities, but they were also angry about the military system that seemed to have turned decent young men into murderers, and by the military's apparent cover-up of the crimes.

The first news of the massacre reached the American public in September 1969, eighteen months after it took place. Earlier in the year, a young American soldier, troubled by the crime, had written to various government officials, including two influential members of Congress. Prodded by the two congressmen, the Army investigated the incident and charged the platoon leader, Lieutenant William L. Calley, Jr., with the murder of a number of Vietnamese civilians. The charges were announced in a small news release. Two months later, after an enterprising journalist made his own investigation, eyewitness stories of the crime, accompanied by photographs, appeared in American newspapers and magazines. The resulting public outcry did much to discredit the war in the eyes of the American people.

The My Lai massacre also revived the question of command responsibility. The Army initially charged fourteen officers, including two generals, with failure to carry out their duty to investigate suspected crimes and to see that the guilty parties were punished. Only two officers actually stood trial, however. They were Lieutenant Calley and Captain Ernest Medina, Calley's immediate superior. Calley was convicted and sentenced to life imprisonment, a sentence that was later reduced to ten years. Medina was acquitted. Despite testimony that Medina ordered the killings, a military court held that the evidence wasn't enough to establish Medina's guilt. In this instance, at least, command responsibility didn't extend beyond the junior officer in charge at the scene of the crime.

American memories of the Vietnam War were revived in August 1990, when Iraq overran its tiny neighbor, Kuwait. President George Bush, calling the invasion "naked aggression," promptly sent American forces to the Persian Gulf to prevent Iraq from advancing into other Middle Eastern countries. Most world leaders agreed with the President's description of the invasion.

The Iraqi leader, Saddam Hussein, insisted, however, that he was merely reclaiming Iraq's own territory.

While some American officials were persuading the United Nations to impose economic restrictions on Iraq and making plans for a military solution if that didn't dislodge the Iraqi forces from Kuwait, other Americans were gathering information for possible use in a trial of the Iraqi leader for war crimes. The charges being considered against Hussein included the use of chemical weapons and the taking of hostages for use as human shields in military installations (both violations of international law) as well as waging a war of aggression.

In February 1991, after a war that lasted only a little more than six weeks, the United States and its allies (with UN approval) freed Kuwait from Iraqi control. Many expected the victory to be followed by an invasion of Iraq and Hussein's capture. When that didn't happen, Hussein brutally suppressed rebellions by Iraqis who opposed his rule. His actions included the destruction of entire villages and the massacre of their residents. The reports of these atrocities and the televised pictures of the miseries of the fleeing survivors resulted in a renewed outcry against Hussein. Nevertheless, Hussein, who remained firmly in control in Iraq, wasn't tried as a war criminal.

In 1991 an outbreak of hostilities in the Balkan Peninsula seemed once again to threaten world peace, as it had in 1914. Modern Yugoslavia was formed after World War I by a union of several Balkan areas having different religions and cultures. Some places had Muslim majorities, while others had Christian Serbian or Croatian majorities. During World War II, the Nazis took over Yugoslavia and divided it into several small states. The country was reunited after World War II as a Communist dictatorship. It wasn't friendly with its larger Communist neighbor, the Soviet Union, however.

Yugoslavian fears of the Soviet Union and the strong rule of the Yugoslavian dictator, Josip Broz Tito, kept the country together in spite of its ethnic and religious animosities. Tito's death in 1980 and the later collapse of the Soviet Union removed these unifying factors, however.

In 1991 several provinces seceded from Yugoslavia. The United Nations and many of its members then recognized them as independent countries. Serbia, which still hoped to rule the entire Balkan Peninsula, attacked the seceding provinces. As the fighting intensified in the former Yugoslavian province of Bosnia-Herzegovina, Serbs and persons of Serbian ancestry made a systematic attempt to force the Muslim residents out of the area. Rape, torture, and massacres were common. Captured soldiers and civilians were held in prison camps under miserable conditions. United Nations officials tried to help civilians in the war zones, but Serbian troops often prevented them from delivering food, medicine, and other supplies.

In August 1992, the UN Security Council condemned the "ethnic cleansing" in Bosnia-Herzegovina as a violation of international law, and followed this action by the creation of a commission to collect evidence of war crimes in that area. Although the Serbs seemed to be responsible for most of the atrocities, the war crimes commission also found evidence that Croatians and Muslims had committed atrocities. In May 1993, the Security Council created an international tribunal with authority to impose prison sentences on those found guilty of war crimes in the Balkans. In September 1993, the UN General Assembly chose eleven judges for the tribunal.

Regardless of the outcome, a new international war crimes trial won't solve the problem of dealing with crimes such as genocide. There is still no permanent

Muslim and Croatian refugees driven from their homes by Serb forces in Bosnia. In 1993 the United Nations named an international tribunal to investigate charges of war crimes in the Bosnian conflict.

world court with authority to try and punish international criminals, and no permanent international peace-keeping force. Moreover, despite the acknowledgment that genocide and aggression are crimes under international law, national sovereignty still protects national leaders who commit these crimes. Bringing them to justice may require military action; criminals must be caught before they can be punished. Some people argue that military intervention is a risky business and should be avoided. Others, troubled by the continuing slaughter in the Balkans and other areas, believe that the risk must be taken.

Meanwhile, every morning at 8:15, the hour when an atomic bomb released its fury on Hiroshima in August 1945, the Peace Clock in that city's Peace Park chimes to remind the world of what once happened there. Halfway around the world, the former concentration camp at Dachau, now a museum, contains a simple monument bearing the words "Never Again." To these words the world's people can add only a fervent "amen." We remain hopeful for the future. We have managed to avoid self-destruction so far. But we wonder. We wonder about the hate that can turn ordinary people into murdering savages. We wonder about the capacity for evildoing that seems to lie in each of us. We wonder about civilization's chance for survival in a world where violence seems to be the rule. We wonder, finally, whether *never* really means what it says.

Appendix A

Defendants at the International Military Tribunal at Nuremberg

Gustav Krupp and Robert Ley, both named in the original indictment, were never tried. Krupp, found unfit to stand trial, died in 1950. Ley committed suicide in October 1945. Those brought to trial were:

Martin Bormann (1900–?)

Head of the Nazi party chancery and personal secretary to Adolf Hitler. Charged with conspiracy, war crimes, and crimes against humanity. Tried *in absentia.* Acquitted of conspiracy charge. Found guilty of other charges. Sentenced to death by hanging. Bormann was never found and presumably died in the final battle for Berlin in 1945.

Karl Doenitz (1891–1980)

Grand admiral and commander in chief of German Navy from 1943 to end of war; headed government briefly after Hitler's death. Charged with conspiracy, crimes against peace, and war crimes. Acquitted of conspiracy charge. Found guilty of other charges. Sentenced to ten years in prison. Released in 1956 after serving full term.

Hans Frank (1900–1946)

Reich commissioner for justice, Reich minister without portfolio, and governor-general of occupied Polish territories. Charged with conspiracy, war crimes, and crimes against humanity. Acquitted of conspiracy charge. Found guilty of other charges. Sentenced to death. Hanged at Nuremberg on October 16, 1946.

Wilhelm Frick (1877–1946)

Reich minister of the interior, Reich minister without portfolio, and Reich protector of Bohemia and Moravia beginning in 1943. Charged with conspiracy, crimes against peace, war crimes, and crimes against humanity. Acquitted of conspiracy charge. Found guilty of other charges. Sentenced to death. Hanged at Nuremberg on October 16, 1946.

Hans Fritzsche (1900–1953)

Head of radio broadcasting in the Reich Ministry of Propaganda from 1942 to end of war. Charged with conspiracy, war crimes, and crimes against humanity. Acquitted of all charges. Later sentenced by a German court to nine years in a labor camp under a German law designed to punish major Nazis. Pardoned in 1950.

Walther Funk (1890–1960)

Reich minister of economics and president of German Reichsbank. Charged with conspiracy, crimes against peace, war crimes, and crimes against humanity. Acquitted of conspiracy charge. Found guilty of other charges. Sentenced to life imprisonment. Released in 1957.

Hermann Goering (1893–1946)

Commander in chief of German Air Force, Reich minister for air, and designated successor to Hitler. Charged with conspiracy, crimes against peace, war crimes, and crimes against humanity. Found guilty of all charges. Sentenced to death. Committed suicide by cyanide poisoning on October 15, 1946.

Rudolf Hess (1894–1987)

Deputy to Hitler, Reich minister without portfolio, and second in line after Goering as Hitler's designated successor. Charged with conspiracy, crimes against peace, war crimes, and crimes against humanity. Acquitted of war crimes and crimes against humanity. Found guilty of other charges. Sentenced to life imprisonment. Committed suicide in prison in 1987.

Alfred Jodl (1890–1946)

Colonel-general and chief of Operations Staff of the German Armed Forces High Command; signed surrender papers in 1945. Charged with conspiracy, crimes against peace, war crimes, and crimes against humanity. Found guilty of all charges. Sentenced to death. Hanged at Nuremberg on October 16, 1946.

Ernst Kaltenbrunner (1903–1946)

Head of the Reich Main Security Office and chief of the Security Police and Security Service. Charged with conspiracy, war crimes, and crimes against humanity. Acquitted of conspiracy charge. Found guilty of other charges. Sentenced to death. Hanged at Nuremberg on October 16, 1946.

Wilhelm Keitel (1882–1946)

Field marshal and chief of the High Command of the German Armed Forces. Charged with conspiracy, crimes against peace, war crimes, and crimes against humanity. Found guilty of all charges. Sentenced to death. Hanged at Nuremberg on October 16, 1946.

Constantin von Neurath (1873–1956)

German foreign minister (1932–1938), then Reich protector of Bohemia and Moravia until 1943. Charged with conspiracy, crimes against peace, war crimes, and crimes against humanity. Found guilty of all charges. Sentenced to fifteen years in prison. Released in 1954.

Franz von Papen (1879–1969)

Reich chancellor (1932), Hitler's vice chancellor (1933–1934), ambassador to Austria (1934–1938), and ambassador to Turkey (1939–1944). Charged with conspiracy and crimes against peace. Acquitted of both charges. Later sentenced by a German court to ten years in a labor camp as a major Nazi offender. Released in 1949 after his sentence was reduced on appeal.

Erich Raeder (1876–1960)

Grand admiral and commander in chief of German Navy until 1943. Charged with conspiracy, crimes against peace, and war crimes. Found guilty of all charges. Sentenced to life imprisonment. Released in 1955.

Joachim von Ribbentrop *(1893–1946)*

German foreign minister (1938–1945). Charged with conspiracy, crimes against peace, war crimes, and crimes against humanity. Found guilty of all charges. Sentenced to death. Hanged at Nuremberg on October 16, 1946.

Alfred Rosenberg *(1893–1946)*

In charge of ideology and foreign policy for the Nazi party and Reich minister for the Eastern Occupied Territories. Charged with conspiracy, crimes against peace, war crimes, and crimes against humanity. Found guilty of all charges. Sentenced to death. Hanged at Nuremberg on October 16, 1946.

Fritz Sauckel *(1894–1946)*

Plenipotentiary-general for Labor Mobilization, which ran the German slave-labor program (1942–1945). Charged with conspiracy, crimes against peace, war crimes, and crimes against humanity. Found guilty of all charges. Sentenced to death. Hanged at Nuremberg on October 16, 1946.

Hjalmar Schacht *(1877–1970)*

Minister of economics (1934–1937), head of the Reichsbank until 1939. Arrested in 1944 as a suspect in a plot against Hitler and held in concentration camps until end of war. Charged with conspiracy and crimes against peace. Acquitted of both charges. Later sentenced by a German court to eight years in a labor camp as a major Nazi offender. Released in 1950 after his conviction was reversed on appeal.

Baldur von Schirach (1907–1974)

Leader of Hitler Youth until 1940, then governor of Vienna. Charged with conspiracy and crimes against humanity. Acquitted of conspiracy charge. Found guilty of crimes against humanity. Sentenced to twenty years in prison. Released in 1966 after serving full term.

Arthur Seyss-Inquart (1892–1946)

Reich minister without portfolio, deputy governor-general of the Polish Occupied Territory, and Reich commissioner for the occupied Netherlands. Charged with conspiracy, crimes against peace, war crimes, and crimes against humanity. Acquitted of conspiracy. Found guilty of other charges. Sentenced to death. Hanged at Nuremberg on October 16, 1946.

Albert Speer (1905–1981)

Reich minister for armaments and war production (1942–1945). Charged with conspiracy, crimes against peace, war crimes, and crimes against humanity. Acquitted of conspiracy and crimes against peace. Found guilty of the other charges. Sentenced to twenty years in prison. Released in 1966 after serving full term.

Julius Streicher (1885–1946)

Local Nazi party leader until 1940; editor of anti-Semitic newspaper *Der Sturmer*. Charged with conspiracy and crimes against humanity. Acquitted of conspiracy. Found guilty of crimes against humanity. Sentenced to death. Hanged at Nuremberg on October 16, 1946.

Appendix B

Twelve Later Nuremberg Trials

Listed in the order in which the indictments were issued. In some cases there was an extended period between the indictments and the opening of the trial.

Medical Case

Defendants: 23 doctors and other medical personnel

Charges: (1) conspiracy to commit war crimes and crimes against humanity; (2) war crimes; (3) crimes against humanity; (4) membership in the SS

Trial dates: December 1946 to July 1947

Judgment announced: August 1947

Verdicts: seven acquittals and sixteen convictions

Sentences: death—seven; life imprisonment—five; 20 years—two; 15 years—one; 10 years—one. The seven sentenced to death were hanged in June 1948. All of the prison sentences were reduced.

Milch Case

Defendant: Erhard Milch, field marshal in German Air Force and member of Central Planning Board, which administered the slave-labor program

Charges: (1) use of slave labor; (2) war crimes; (3) crimes against humanity

Trial dates: January to March 1947

Judgment announced: April 1947

Verdict: convicted of using slave labor

Sentence: life imprisonment, later reduced to 15 years

Justice Case

Defendants: 14 lawyers, judges, and other officials of German Ministry of Justice

Charges: (1) conspiracy to commit war crimes and crimes against humanity; (2) war crimes; (3) crimes against humanity; (4) membership in the SS

Trial dates: March to October 1947

Judgment announced: December 1947

Verdicts: four acquittals and ten convictions

Sentences: life imprisonment—four; 10 years—four; 7 years—one; 5 years—one. Most sentences were later reduced.

Pohl Case

Defendants: 18 administrators of concentration camps and SS-owned businesses that used inmates as slave labor

Charges: (1) conspiracy to commit war crimes and crimes against humanity; (2) war crimes; (3) crimes against humanity; (4) membership in the SS

Trial dates: April to September 1947

Judgment announced: November 1947

Verdicts: three acquittals and fifteen convictions

Sentences: death—four, including the principal defendant, Oswald Pohl; life imprisonment—three; 25 years—one; 20 years—one; 10 years—six. Pohl was hanged in June 1951. All other sentences were reduced.

Flick Case

Defendants: 6 officials in the Flick combine

Charges: (1) use of slave labor; (2) spoliation (plunder or wanton destruction of property); (3) crimes against humanity during the prewar period; (4) cooperation with the SS in its criminal activities; (5) membership in the SS

Trial dates: April to November 1947

Judgment announced: December 1947

Verdicts: three acquittals and three convictions

Sentences: 7 years—one (the principal defendant, Friedrich Flick); 5 years—one; 2½ years—one

Farben Case

Defendants: 23 officials in the I. G. Farben combine

Charges: (1) planning and waging aggressive war; (2) spoliation; (3) use of slave labor; (4) membership in the SS; (5) conspiracy to wage aggressive war

Trial dates: August 1947 to June 1948

Judgment announced: July 1948

Verdicts: ten acquittals and thirteen convictions

Sentences: 8 years—two; 7 years—one; 6 years—three; 5 years—one; 4 years—one; 3 years—one; 2 years—two; 1 ½ years—two

Hostages Case

Defendants: 10 field marshals or generals in the German Army

Charges: (1) mass murder; (2) spoliation; (3) illegal executions; (4) use of slave labor

Trial dates: July 1947 to February 1948

Judgment announced: February 1948

Verdicts: two acquittals and eight convictions

Sentences: life imprisonment—two; 20 years—two; 15 years—one; 12 years—one; 10 years—one; 7 years—one. Most of these sentences were later reduced.

RuSHA Case

Defendants: 14 officials in the SS Main Race and Resettlement Office and related organizations

Charges: (1) crimes against humanity; (2) war crimes; (3) membership in the SS

Trial dates: October 1947 to February 1948

Judgment announced: March 1948

Verdicts: one acquittal and thirteen convictions

Sentences: life imprisonment—one; 25 years—two; 20 years—one; 15 years—three; 10 years—one; time already served—five. Most sentences were later reduced.

Einsatzgruppen Case

Defendants: 22 members of the SS Einsatzgruppen, or special squads that accompanied the German Army

Charges: (1) crimes against humanity; (2) war crimes; (3) membership in the SS

Trial dates: October 1947 to February 1948

Judgment announced: April 1948

Verdicts: all defendants convicted of one or more charges

Sentences: death—fourteen, including the principal defendant, Otto Ohlendorf; life imprisonment—two; 20 years—three; 10 years—two; time already served— one. Ohlendorf was hanged in June 1951. The other sentences were reduced.

Krupp Case

Defendants: 12 executives in the Krupp armaments firm

Charges: (1) crimes against peace; (2) spoliation; (3) use of slave labor; (4) conspiracy to commit crimes against peace

Trial dates: December 1947 to June 1948

Judgment announced: July 1948

Verdicts: one acquittal and eleven convictions

Sentences: 12 years—three, including the principal defendant, Alfried Krupp, whose property was also ordered to be confiscated; 10 years—two; 9 years—two; 7 years—one; 6 years—two; time already served—one. Most of these sentences were later reduced.

Ministries Case

Defendants: 21 high-ranking officials of various German government ministries

Charges: (1) planning, initiating, and waging aggressive war; (2) conspiracy to commit crimes against peace; (3) murder and mistreatment of war prisoners; (4) atrocities against Germans during the prewar period; (5) atrocities against other civilians; (6) spoliation; (7) use of slave labor; (8) membership in the SS

Trial dates: January to November 1948

Judgment announced: April 1949

Verdicts: two acquittals and nineteen convictions

Sentences: 25 years—one; 20 years—two; 15 years—three; 10 years—two; 7 years—six; 6 years—one; 5 years—two; 4 years—one; time already served—one. Many of these sentences were later reduced.

High Command Case

Defendants: 13 high-level command or staff officers in the German armed forces

Charges: (1) planning and waging aggressive war; (2) war crimes and crimes against humanity involving enemy belligerents and prisoners of war; (3) war crimes and crimes against humanity involving civilians; (4) conspiracy

Trial dates: February to August 1948

Judgment announced: October 1948

Verdicts: two acquittals and eleven convictions

Sentences: life imprisonment—two; 20 years—three; 15 years—two; 8 years—one; 7 years—one; 5 years—one; time already served—one. Some sentences were later reduced.

Appendix C

Defendants at the International Military Tribunal at Tokyo

Two defendants died during the trial: Yosuke Matsuoka, in June 1946, and Admiral Osami Nagano, in January 1947. A third defendant, Shumei Okawa, was held mentally unfit to stand trial. He was released from a mental hospital in December 1948 and died in 1957. The other defendants, all of whom were convicted of at least one charge, were:

Sadao Araki (1877–1966)

General in Japanese Army, war minister (1931–1934), education minister 1938 and 1939. Convicted of conspiracy and waging aggressive war. Sentenced to life imprisonment. Paroled in 1955. Released from parole requirements in 1958.

Kenji Doihara (1883–1948)

General in Japanese Army. Involved in 1931 bombing at Mukden; commanded troops in Manchuria (1938–

1940) and in Singapore (1944, 1945). Convicted of conspiracy, waging aggressive war, and ordering, authorizing, or permitting atrocities. Sentenced to death. Hanged on December 23, 1948.

Kingoro Hashimoto (1890–1957)

Colonel in Japanese Army. Involved in Mukden incident, Rape of Nanking, and sinking of *Panay*. Convicted of conspiracy and waging aggressive war. Sentenced to life imprisonment. Paroled in 1955.

Shunroku Hata (1879–1962)

Field marshal in Japanese Army, war minister (1939, 1940), commanded troops in China (1938, 1941–1944). Convicted of conspiracy, waging aggressive war, and disregarding his duty to prevent atrocities. Sentenced to life imprisonment. Paroled in 1954. Released from parole requirements in 1958.

Kiichiro Hiranuma (1867–1952)

Prime minister (1938), minister of home affairs and minister without portfolio (1940, 1941). Became president of Privy Council in 1945. Convicted of conspiracy and waging aggressive war. Sentenced to life imprisonment. Died while serving sentence.

Koki Hirota (1878–1948)

Foreign minister (1933–March 1936, June 1937–May 1938), prime minister (March 1936–February 1937). Convicted of conspiracy, waging aggressive war, and disregarding his duty to prevent atrocities. Sentenced to death. Hanged on December 23, 1948.

Naoki Hoshino (1892–1978)

Official of Japanese government in Manchuria (1932–1940), minister without portfolio (July 1940–April 1941), chief cabinet secretary (October 1941–July 1944). Convicted of conspiracy and waging aggressive war. Sentenced to life imprisonment. Paroled in 1955. Released from parole requirements in 1958.

Seishiro Itagaki (1885–1948)

General in Japanese Army, war minister (1938, 1939), army chief of staff in China (1939–1941), then commanded troops in Korea and Singapore. Convicted of conspiracy, waging aggressive war, and ordering or permitting atrocities. Sentenced to death. Hanged on December 23, 1948.

Okinori Kaya (1889–1977)

Minister of finance (June 1937–May 1938, October 1941–February 1944). Convicted of conspiracy and waging aggressive war. Sentenced to life imprisonment. Paroled in 1955. Released from parole requirements in 1958.

Koichi Kido (1889–1977)

Chief secretary to the Lord Keeper of the Privy Seal (1930–1937), education minister (1937), welfare minister (1938), minister of home affairs (1939), Lord Keeper of the Privy Seal (1940–1945). Convicted of conspiracy and waging aggressive war. Sentenced to life imprisonment. Paroled in 1955. Released from parole requirements in 1958.

Heitaro Kimura (1888–1948)

General in Japanese Army, vice minister of war (April 1941–March 1943), commanded troops in Burma (1944, 1945). Convicted of conspiracy, waging aggressive war, ordering or permitting atrocities, and disregarding his duty to prevent atrocities. Sentenced to death. Hanged on December 23, 1948.

Kuniaki Koiso (1880–1950)

General in Japanese Army, overseas minister (1939, 1940), governor-general of Korea (May 1942–July 1944), prime minister (July 1944–April 1945). Convicted of conspiracy, waging aggressive war, and disregarding his duty to prevent atrocities. Sentenced to life imprisonment. Died while serving sentence.

Iwane Matsui (1878–1948)

General in Japanese Army, emperor's personal representative at Geneva disarmament conference (1932–1937), commanded Japanese army in central China (October 1937–February 1938), then retired. One of two defendants acquitted of conspiracy charge, and one of three acquitted of aggressive war charge. Convicted of disregarding his duty to prevent atrocities. Sentenced to death. Hanged on December 23, 1948.

Jiro Minami (1874–1955)

General in Japanese Army, war minister (1931), commander of Japanese army in Manchuria (1934–1936), governor-general of Korea (1936–1942), member of Privy Council (1942–1945). Convicted of conspiracy and waging aggressive war. Sentenced to life imprisonment. Paroled in 1954.

Akira Muto (1892–1948)

General in Japanese Army, chief of Military Affairs Bureau in war ministry (1939–1942), held staff or command positions in China, Southeast Asia, and the Philippines during the 1930s and 1940s. Convicted of conspiracy, waging aggressive war, ordering or permitting atrocities, and disregarding his duty to prevent atrocities. Sentenced to death. Hanged on December 23, 1948.

Takasumi Oka (1890–1973)

Admiral in Japanese Navy, chief of General and Military Affairs Bureau in Navy ministry (1940–1944), vice minister of Navy (1944). Convicted of conspiracy and waging aggressive war. Sentenced to life imprisonment. Paroled in 1954. Released from parole requirements in 1958.

Hiroshi Oshima (1886–1975)

General in Japanese Army, ambassador to Germany (1938, 1939, and December 1940–April 1945). Helped to arrange Japan's wartime alliance with Germany and Italy. One of three defendants acquitted of aggressive war charge. Convicted of conspiracy. Sentenced to life imprisonment. Paroled in 1955. Released from parole requirements in 1958.

Kenryo Sato (1895–1975)

General in Japanese Army, chief of Military Affairs Bureau (1942–1944), commanded troops in Southeast Asia in 1945. Convicted of conspiracy and waging aggressive war. Sentenced to life imprisonment. Paroled in 1956, the last Class A war criminal to be released from prison. Released from parole requirements in 1958.

Mamoru Shigemitsu (1887–1957)

Ambassador to China, the Soviet Union, and Great Britain during the prewar period; foreign minister (1943–1945); signed surrender papers in September 1945. One of two defendants acquitted of conspiracy charge. Convicted of waging aggressive war and disregarding his duty to prevent atrocities. Sentenced to seven years in prison. Paroled in 1950. Later served as foreign minister, when he helped to arrange the release of other Class A defendants.

Shigetaro Shimada (1883–1976)

Admiral in Japanese Navy, Navy minister (1941–1944). Convicted of conspiracy and waging aggressive war. Sentenced to life imprisonment. Paroled in 1955. Released from parole requirements in 1958.

Toshio Shiratori (1887–1949)

Ambassador to Italy (1938–1940); helped to arrange Japan's wartime alliance with Italy and Germany. One of three defendants acquitted of aggressive war charge. Convicted of conspiracy. Sentenced to life imprisonment. Died while serving sentence.

Teiichi Suzuki (1888–1989)

General in Japanese Army. Minister without portfolio and president of Cabinet Planning Board (1941–1943).

Convicted of conspiracy and waging aggressive war. Sentenced to life imprisonment. Paroled in 1955. Released from parole requirements in 1958.

Shigenori Togo (1884–1950)

Foreign minister (October 1941–September 1942 and again in 1945). Convicted of conspiracy and waging aggressive war. Sentenced to twenty years in prison. Died while serving sentence.

Hideki Tojo (1884–1948)

General in Japanese Army, served in Manchuria (1935–1938) and as vice minister of war (1938), war minister (1940–July 1944), and prime minister (October 1941–July 1944). Convicted of conspiracy, waging aggressive war, and ordering or permitting atrocities. Sentenced to death. Hanged on December 23, 1948.

Yoshijiro Umezu (1882–1949)

General in Japanese Army; commanded troops in Manchuria and other parts of China; vice war minister (1936–1938); chief of staff from July 1944 to end of war. Signed surrender papers in September 1945. Convicted of conspiracy and waging aggressive war. Sentenced to life imprisonment. Died while serving sentence.

Notes

1. *Time,* April 30, 1945, pp. 38–46.

2. *Encyclopedia Americana,* International Edition (Danbury, CT: Grolier Inc., 1993), article on World War I.

3. Quoted in Arthur Schlesinger, Jr., ed., *The Dynamics of World Power: A Documentary History of U.S. Foreign Policy 1945–1973* (New York: Chelsea House Publishers, 1973), Vol. 1, p. 449.

4. John Mendelsohn, "War Crimes Trials and Clemency in Germany and Japan," *Americans as Proconsuls: U.S. Military Government in Germany and Japan, 1944–1952* (Carbondale: Southern Illinois University Press, 1984), p. 228.

5. *Time,* May 20, 1946, p. 24.

6. Philip R. Piccigallo, *The Japanese on Trial* (Austin: University of Texas Press, 1979), p. 95.

7. Ibid.

8. Thomas L. Karsten and James H. Mathias, "The Judgment at Nuremberg," *The New Republic,* October 21, 1946.

Bibliography

Starred books are recommended for young adult readers.

Germany

Bird, Kai. *The Chairman: John J. McCloy, the Making of the American Establishment.* New York: Simon & Schuster, 1992.

Bosch, William J. *Judgment on Nuremberg: American Attitudes Toward the Major German War-Crimes Trials.* Chapel Hill: University of North Carolina Press, 1970.

Bower, Tom. *The Pledge Betrayed.* Garden City, N.Y.: Doubleday & Co., 1982.

Harris, Whitney R. *Tyranny on Trial.* Dallas: Southern Methodist University Press, 1954.

Knieriem, August. *The Nuremberg Trials.* Chicago: Henry Regnery Co., 1959 (trans. from German).

*Neave, Airey. *On Trial at Nuremberg.* Boston: Little, Brown & Co., 1978.

Read, Anthony, and David Fisher. *The Fall of Berlin*. New York: W. W. Norton & Co., 1992.

*Shirer, William L. *The Rise and Fall of the Third Reich*. New York: Ballantine Books, 1983 (published originally by Simon & Schuster, 1950).

Taylor, Telford. *Nuremberg Trials: War Crimes and International Law*. New York: Carnegie Endowment for International Peace, 1949.

*————. *The Anatomy of the Nuremberg Trials*. New York: Alfred A. Knopf, 1992.

Tusa, Ann and John. *The Nuremberg Trials*. New York: Atheneum, 1984.

Whiting, Charles. *Massacre at Malmédy*. New York: Stein & Day, 1971.

Zink, Harold. *The United States in Germany, 1944–1955*. Princeton: D. Van Nostrand Co., 1957.

Transcript of trial before IMT at Nuremberg: Vol. 1, for individual indictments; Vol. 22, for individual verdicts

Japan

Behr, Edward. *Hirohito: Behind the Myth*. New York: Vintage Books, 1990.

Beser, Jacob. *Hiroshima and Nagasaki Revisited*. Memphis: Global Press, 1988.

*Brackman, Arnold C. *The Other Nuremberg: The Untold Story of the Tokyo War Crimes Trials*. New York: William Morrow & Co., 1987.

Buckley, Roger. *Occupation Diplomacy: Britain, the United States and Japan 1945–1952*. Cambridge: Cambridge University Press, 1982.

Cox, Alvin D. *Tojo*. New York: Ballantine Books, 1975.

Finn, Richard B. *Winners in Peace: MacArthur, Yoshida, and Postwar Japan.* Berkeley: University of California Press, 1992.

Horwitz, Solis. "The Tokyo Trial." *International Conciliation,* November 1950.

*Lael, Richard L. *The Yamashita Precedent: War Crimes and Command Responsibility.* Wilmington, Del.: Scholarly Resources, Inc., 1982.

*Minear, Richard H. *Victors' Justice: The Tokyo War Crimes Trial.* Princeton: Princeton University Press, 1971.

Oka, Yoshitake. *Konoe Fumimaro: A Political Biography.* Tokyo: University of Tokyo Press, 1983 (trans. from Japanese).

Perry, John Curtis. *Beneath the Eagle's Wings: Americans in Occupied Japan.* New York: Dodd, Mead & Co., 1980.

*Piccigallo, Philip R. *The Japanese on Trial.* Austin: University of Texas Press, 1979.

Schaller, Michael. *Douglas MacArthur: The Far Eastern General.* New York: Oxford University Press, 1989.

Sheldon, Walt. *The Honorable Conquerors: The Occupation of Japan, 1945–1952.* New York: Macmillan Co., 1965.

Sigal, Leon V. *Fighting to a Finish: The Politics of War Termination in the United States and Japan, 1945.* Ithaca: Cornell University Press, 1988.

Takeda, Kiyoko. *The Dual Image of the Japanese Emperor.* New York: New York University Press, 1988.

Taylor, Lawrence. *A Trial of Generals: Homma, Yamashita, MacArthur.* South Bend, Ind.: Icarus Press, 1981.

General

*Appleman, John A. *Military Tribunals and International Crimes.* Westport, Ct.: Greenwood Press, 1971 (published originally by Bobbs-Merrill, 1954).

Facts on File, 1945–1958, 1971–1992.

Foreign Relations of the United States, Vol. 6, 1945, Vol. 8, 1946, Vol. 6, 1948.

Mendelsohn, John. "War Crimes Trials and Clemency in Germany and Japan." In *Americans as Proconsuls: U.S. Military Government in Germany and Japan, 1944–1952,* Robert Wolfe, ed. Carbondale: Southern Illinois University Press, 1984.

New York Times Index, 1945–1958. Also *Times* articles on recent events in Persian Gulf and Yugoslavia.

Time, various articles, 1945 ff., especially April 30, 1945, for description of Buchenwald in Chapter 1, and December 5, 1969, for information on discovery of My Lai massacre.

Index